THE CREATION OF WEALTH

D0932818

THE CREATION OF WEALTH

*Recovering a Christian Understanding
of Money, Work, and Ethics*

Fred Catherwood

CROSSWAY BOOKS

A DIVISION OF
GOOD NEWS PUBLISHERS
WHEATON, ILLINOIS

Library of Congress Cataloging-in-Publication Data
Catherwood, H. F. R. (Henry Frederick Ross), Sir, 1925–
   The creation of wealth : Recovering a Christian understanding of
money, work, and ethics / Fred Catherwood.
     p. cm.
   Includes index.
   ISBN 1-58134-352-3 (pbk. : alk. paper)
   1. Christianity and economics. 2. Christianity and politics. I. Title.
BR115.E3 C33   2002
261.8'5—dc21   2002005323

VP		13	12	11	10	09	08	07	06	05	04	03	02
15	14	13	12	11	10	9	8	7	6	5	4	3	2	1

CONTENTS

PREFACE

The human disaster of 9/11 and the Enron and other major scandals in the following year both undermine two basic assumptions of our secular society: first, that there is no absolute good and evil; and second, that there is no need of a moral order of right and wrong to underpin the precise legalities of the civil law. It is time we looked again at the moral order we have lost, at the Christian beliefs that made our society great.

It was not a canon of civil law or rules of political correctness that made America great or that created the democracy and wealth of the West. It is easy to see why Christian respect for the dignity of the individual could lead to democracy; but why, when Christians are taught not to set their hearts on riches, is Western society ten times richer than the rest of the world? Why, too, after half a century of aid, have poor countries not even begun to catch up?

Comparative wealth seems to have little to do with the possession of natural resources. North America and Latin America both have plenty of natural resources, but one is much richer than the other. Switzerland and Holland are both small countries with few natural resources but are both among the richest in the world. They have their own explanations. The Swiss say, "God gave us only rock, snow, and ice." The Dutch say, "God gave us only sea, sand, and wind." "But," both say, "he gave us John Calvin, and that was enough."

I used to wonder why, within Christendom, Protestant countries seem to be richer than Catholic countries. After all, the essential split was theological, between salvation through sacraments and salvation by faith alone. Why should that make any difference economically?

To find the answer, we have to look at the causes of the explosive economic growth of the last four centuries, that sprang up on both sides of the Atlantic wherever the new Protestant churches were dominant. In the sixteenth century, Luther in Germany, Zwingli in Switzerland, and Calvin in France contrasted the teaching of the medieval church with the teaching of the apostles. At about the same time as the Bible was translated out of Latin into the common languages, Gutenberg invented the printing press. These two innovations put affordable Bibles into the hands of opinion leaders across Protestant Europe, and the direct words of Christ and the apostles became the basis of the new Protestant creeds and the final authority for the individual Christian.

The great Bible commentaries of John Calvin showed how one part of the Bible fitted with the other, and his *Institutes of the Christian Religion* summarized the doctrines of the new Protestant churches. But ordinary Christians also read the Bible for themselves. They read Christ's teaching that every single one of us has talents, and that, whether those talents be few or many, we have a duty to multiply them; Christ's judgment on those who buried their God-given talents was severe (Matt. 25:26-30). They read the apostle Paul's commands, "If a man will not work, he shall not eat" (2 Thess. 3:10); and that Christians were to "redeem the time" (Eph. 5:16; Col. 4:5, KJV) and not waste it. They read all the wisdom of Solomon about "fools" and "the wise," and soon they developed a way of life in sharp contrast to that of the medieval aristocracy, who squandered their wealth in building great houses that needed an army of servants. Protestantism became a creed of hard work and steady development of skills, and of saving and investing rather than spending. Its mark was self-discipline; and on the battlefield, a real test of personal discipline, Cromwell's New Model Army broke the undisciplined charges of Prince Rupert's swashbuckling Cavaliers.

Christ taught, "let your 'Yes' be 'Yes,' and your 'No,' 'No'" (Matt. 5:37). Truth is the cement of all human relations; and Christians, above all, must be able to trust each other. Trade moved from bazaar bargaining for short-term profits, to long-term relationships between merchants who knew they could trust each other. Savings from a far wider range of people were deposited in the new banks, which had earned their trust, and those savings gave a solid base for the expansion of investment and trade. When King Louis XIV expelled the French Protestants, the Huguenots, in 1685, all their trading relationships remained intact and they simply moved their business base from France to one of the welcoming Protestant countries. The economic rise of Prussia, Holland, England, and New England was greatly helped by their arrival; meanwhile France, until then the richest country in Europe, went into long-term decline.

The most spectacular and the best-documented change was the introduction of the "scientific method." In the early seventeenth century the English Lord Chancellor Sir Francis Bacon spelled out its logic, and in the second half of the century it was institutionalized in the "Royal Society." Until then, science had been under the wing of the church, which had adopted the scientific theories of the ancient Greeks. But the new Protestants, reading the "book of God's word," decided that they should be guided not by intellectual theory but by studying nature, which Bacon called "the book of God's works." No scientific theory should be accepted unless tested and proved against nature. What Galileo actually saw through his telescope was more important than the theories of the most brilliant minds.

Their starting point was that God's creation must reflect his nature as the Bible had revealed it. He was the one and only God, so the laws of nature would be the same wherever we found them. He was a God of order, so we would find order in nature; a God of reason, who argued cause and effect, so we would find a rational relation between the laws of nature. And God had promised Noah, after the flood, that the laws of nature would be stable until the end of time (Gen. 8:20-22). We were the trustees of nature, which a good God had given, in Bacon's words, "for the relief of man's estate." So we had a duty to develop natural science for human benefit. As one writer described Bacon's thoughts, "Investigations were to be conducted into secondary causes with utilitarian ends in mind."

The study of "origins" was specifically excluded from the new scientific method, because it presumed to inquire into what God, in his wisdom, had not revealed.

We have only to contrast this worldview with the rising pagan view of the natural world today, to realize how specifically Christian is the scientific method. The pagan has many gods, all of them fierce; and nature is hostile, disorderly, irrational, unstable, and malign—views reflected in today's art. Fringes of the "Green" movement see nature itself as divine and untouchable. But the greatest danger to the advance of science is that it has lost its moral roots. The development of science is no longer "for the relief of man's estate." It can be used to kill as well as to cure, to dominate other countries and cultures rather than to support them. The "man in the white coat" has become a sinister figure. Science has been associated with the theory of "the survival of the fittest," the idea that was used in support of the two tyrannical ideologies of the twentieth century, communism and fascism. Christians need to place science once again in its divine framework, where it must be "for the relief of man's estate."

Not only science is in danger with the Christian ethic under attack, so are the other Christian beliefs that powered the West to its present wealth. The institution that most exactly reflected the Christian ethic was the learned profession. It aimed to advance the state of knowledge with every new generation, to make that knowledge serve the community, to maintain a professional code of ethics and exclude anyone who failed to keep to it. We have come to rely on the professional standards of medicine for our health, of civil engineers for our roads, of aeronautical engineers to keep us safe in the sky, and of public accountants to see that the accounts of the corporations in which we invest our money are true and fair—until the professional auditors of Enron were found to have shredded their clients' incriminating documents. Like the pain of toothache, that lapse is a warning of hidden corruption that has to be put right as fast as can be.

The problem is not just the greed of the "independent" auditors or of the executives who ran Enron. The executives were under pressure, like all companies quoted on the stock exchange, to show a brisk increase in each quarter's profits. We live in a materialistic and greedy society, far removed from the beliefs that powered the rise of the West. We are not satisfied with steady dividends; we want to get rich quick, so we put our brokers under pressure, they put the pension funds under pressure, and they pressure the companies they own.

In both Britain and America, greed is financed by growing trade deficits. The growth of demand can no longer be met by what we produce ourselves and has to be met instead by imports from other countries. So the growing excess of our imports over our exports has to be financed by borrowing from the Japanese and other countries that also export more than they import. The deficit is now too large to be ignored.

Under the *International Herald Tribune*'s headline "Widening

Trade Gap May Sink US Currency" (May 4, 2002), Eric Pfanner writes, "The yawning US current account deficit, the broadest measure of the shortfall between the value of the goods and services which America sends overseas, compared with those it buys from abroad, periodically surfaces as Exhibit A on some economists' lists of reasons the US economy and the dollar are headed for twin collapses." He quotes Stephen Roach, chief economist at Morgan Stanley: "America's ever-widening current account deficit is on an inherently unstable path. A correction is coming, it is just a question of when the denial finally cracks." Pfanner comments, "If imports persistently outpace exports—and last year they did to the amount of $417 billion—the US economy is essentially living on borrowed time, mortgaging its future to foreigners who have been willing, for now, to finance America's fling with consumption. The surplus of [foreign] investment, these economists say, is piling up like a huge debt that eventually has to be paid back."

For the moment, the markets are used to the dollar and comfortable with its management by the Federal Reserve Bank in Washington; and there has been, until now, no alternative global currency. But, given a drop in confidence in the dollar, there is, for the first time, an alternative currency. The euro is now the official currency of eleven members of the European Union, including Germany, France, Spain, Italy, and Holland, with a population only 14 percent less than that of the United States, and a steady trade surplus. These eleven countries are often referred to as the "Eurozone." If greed presses too far and confidence cracks, a slide from the dollar is now only too easy.

The deficit is an economic problem that may be put right in time. But the loss of any sense of right and wrong is far more serious. The greatness of the West was built on its Christian faith, which gave our nations a moral order, telling us what was right and what was wrong. Now our new moral mentors tell us there is no absolute right and no absolute wrong. But how can we believe that after the cold-blooded murder of three thousand people on 9/11? And how can we throw over all the beliefs that have powered the success of the West?

The central argument of secular humanism is that no one's faith can claim that it is true. Therefore secular humanism's interpretation of religious liberty is that no one faith has any unique right to the public space in schools, universities, or anywhere else—that is, no faith except its own, because secular humanism is itself a faith and is intolerant of any other.

The Christian belief is that church and state are complementary. "Give to Caesar what is Caesar's, and to God what is God's" (Matt. 22:21). The church did not demand official recognition by the Roman Empire; it earned it by the behavior of Christians who were good and helpful neighbors, and by the good civic sense of its teaching. When the Roman Empire fell, the Christian church survived and earned the respect of the pagan tribes who, one by one, gave up their gods and were baptized as Christians. When, in its medieval arrogance, the church claimed the political power of the state, it became corrupt.

The right course for Christians is to "earn our way back" to that place of respect by taking care of the many human problems that have been created by the secular humanistic agenda, including the breakup of the family, the drug culture, the rise in crime, and the neglect of the poor. I hope that this book will show how vital the Christian moral order is, and why our countries must never neglect it.

Looking again at *The Christian in Industrial Society,* which I wrote a generation ago—the second and last American edition, *On the Job,* came out in 1983—those times seemed more innocent and optimistic. True, some problems seem to have melted; there seem to be fewer labor disputes, the threat of communism has gone, and the market economy is now accepted worldwide.

But it is not enough to get rid of what was bad. If we do not want something worse, we have to put back in place all that was good. This book is about the core beliefs that made the Western world and how we can put them into practice today.

Chapter 1 looks at the "Protestant work ethic," which lifted the Bible-reading countries up by their own bootstraps through hard work, saving and investment, and development of their talents.

Chapter 2 shows how the new spirit of trust spurred trade and deposit banking and, over three hundred years, gave the West the great wealth that a growing lack of trust now puts at risk.

Chapter 3 looks at the legitimate place of government in our society and the need to separate church and state so that the church and not the state lays down the moral law.

Chapter 4 argues that democracy gives the needed swift feedback mechanism to an industrial society, but that it is no longer "for the people" but for the fundraisers who decide the candidates.

Chapter 5 looks at the case for competition in business but also at the need to prevent the development of unfair competition by big companies against the small.

Chapter 6 looks at the stock market boom and bust, at the snarling of prosperity by unrestrained greed, and argues that business needs moral moorings.

Chapter 7 shows the vast improvements that global trade brings to some and the swift disaster it brings to others, the power of the new global corporations, the grip of corruption on poor economies, and the real danger that this corruption will feed back into the West.

Chapter 8 looks at the electronic economy, which enables money to flash around the world at the speed of light, driving currency flows out of control and plunging stock markets into crisis.

Chapter 9 considers the leadership qualities needed in our swiftly changing world to recover the virtues that gave the West its leadership and greatness. The role models we will look at commanded the trust required to lead, the experience and knowledge to deal with the problems, and, above all, the faith and guidelines to keep steady in the worst crisis.

1

WORK

"If a man will not work, he shall not eat."
THE APOSTLE PAUL (2 THESS. 3:10)

"A country, even a rich one, that fails to provide gainful employment for the many, is failing in its basic task."
THE WASHINGTON POST

"The professional should always determine himself what his work should be and what good work is."
PETER DRUCKER

How did the West become so rich? Why have illegal immigrants from all of Latin America poured over the Rio Grande? Why do others risk death by crossing from Africa to Spain on rough seas in tiny boats? Why do still others risk suffocation by hiding in trucks to cross the English Channel? It is because wages in the industrial democracies are ten times those in the rest of the world.

Development aid aims to get poorer countries to the point of economic takeoff. Money pours in for dams, roads, harbors, power stations, farm and industrial development, and, so development theory goes, free markets will look after the rest. But it hasn't worked out like that. Even if they have gotten somewhat better, the ten-to-one ratio is still there. And a lot of those poorer countries have become worse.

It is not just the great natural resources of the United States that has brought it riches. It is the vigorous, intelligent, and systematic development of those resources. South America has equal natural resources, but most South Americans are still desperately poor.

There is not much doubt about the starting point of Western economic development. From the seventeenth century on there has been the greatest explosion of knowledge, trade, and wealth in recorded history. The important question is, why did it come just then, and why in the Western culture and not, say, in the cultures of the East or of Islam?

Though Western expansion has gone so well, we still need to ask these questions, because we are surrounded by failed and unhealthy societies and, unless we know what has driven our success, we could catch their infection, and our prosperity could sicken and die.

WHAT TRIGGERED THE EXPLOSION?

Let's go back to find the vital chemistry that put the West on its course to wealth.

In the hundred years before the Pilgrim fathers set out for America, there were two events that changed the culture of Europe. The first was the translation of the Bible, the foundation document of Europe's Christian faith, from Latin into Europe's commonly spoken languages. The second was the invention of printing, which enabled this newly translated book and the teachings based on it to circulate far and wide.

Just as it did in its very earliest days (see Acts 17:6), so throughout the first millennium of the Christian era the church "turned the world upside down." The neighborly love and simple lifestyle of Christians converted the Roman Empire, and when that great empire fell, they founded mission stations among the invading tribes to look after the sick, the old, and the traveler, and to educate the young. Slowly, this simple Christian love converted the barbarian tribes that had overthrown Rome—the Goths, Lombards, Franks, Angles, Saxons, Danes, and Slavs—and they were the ancestors of the Western world.

But as it moved into the second millennium, the church became rich and politically powerful. It was the age of prince-bishops; great castles were matched by great cathedrals; and as the official church strayed far from the simple message of Jesus and the apostles, the Bible was kept well away from the people, and politically dangerous "heretics" were persecuted by an unholy alliance of church and state.

The attack of the Reformer Martin Luther was theological. The church, he said, had no right to ask for money for the forgiveness of sins. Since God alone could forgive sins, and forgiveness was through faith alone, the church's works of penance were not needed. The second wave of Reformers, led by a French lawyer, John Calvin, began the job of building the new foundations of the Reformed church, based on the teaching of Jesus and the apostles. And their teaching was from a Bible that most of their congregations were now reading for themselves.

THE NEW WORLDVIEW

The new worldview that emerged from the reading of the Bible was markedly different from that of the medieval church, which had seen the physical world as evil. The saints of the medieval church were withdrawn from the commerce of life and did not marry or trade. Spirituality was to be found in the holy ground of the monastery or convent and by the practice of religious rites. The new Bible-reading generation found that the natural resources of the world were not evil but were created by a good God for our use, and that God had put us in charge of them. "Let them have dominion over the fish of the sea, and over the birds of the air, and over the cattle, and over all the earth" (Gen. 1:26, RSV).

Fast-forward two millennia to the songs of King David:

> When I look at thy heavens, the work of thy fingers, the moon and the stars which thou hast established, what is man that thou art mindful of him?

Then he answers his own question:

> Thou hast given him dominion over the works of thy hands; thou hast put all things under his feet (Ps. 8:3, 6, RSV).

The realization by the Reformers that this "dominion" over creation included all Christians, not just their leaders, brought with it three great changes: the growth of democracy and the growth of applied science, both of which were backed by an ethic of hard work, innovation, and saving. These changes transformed Protestant commerce and industry.

THE NEW WORK ETHIC

The new work ethic taught that work is part of the divine order and is a prime purpose of our lives. Lack of useful employment removes our meaning and purpose. That is why, as the quote at the chapter head from the *Washington Post* says, society must make sure that there is employment for everyone. The same ideal is inscribed more permanently on the Franklin Roosevelt memorial in Washington.

The New Testament says a great deal about our attitude to our daily work. Paul tells the Colossians (3:22-24),

Slaves, obey your earthly masters in everything; and do it, not only when their eye is on you, but with sincerity of heart and reverence for the Lord. Whatever you do, work at it with all your heart, as working for the Lord and not for men. . . . It is the Lord Christ you are serving.

If that is true for a slave, how much more is it true for those who are free and are paid for their work? Paul tells the Thessalonians in his first letter (4:11-12),

Make it your ambition to lead a quiet life, to mind your own business and to work with your hands, just as we told you, so that your daily life may win the respect of outsiders and so that you will not be dependent on anybody.

As congregations began to read the Bible for themselves, what sprang out of the print was the importance to God of the life and work of the ordinary Christian. All men and women were made "in the image of God," and all Christians had an individual "calling" for which God had gifted them. The Christian faith was more than the "you shall not" of the Ten Commandments; it was direct, personal answerability to God for the full development and use of the talents he had given.

As we have seen, this is spelled out most clearly in Christ's parables of the talents (Matt. 25:14-28) and of the pounds (Luke 19:11-26). In both, the master insists that each servant must multiply the talents he had been given; and in each parable, the master praises those who have done so, saying, "Well done, good and faithful servant." But the master sweeps away the excuses of the servant who had done nothing with his talent: "You wicked, lazy servant!" (Matt. 25:26).

So it is not enough just to pick up a job and do it as it has always been done before. We have to bite off more than we can chew—and then find a way to chew it. Christians cannot relax as soon as they have enough money or as soon as they have mastered a job. They have a duty to train themselves and develop their abilities to the limit that their other God-given duties to family and church allow.

DEMOCRACY AND THE DIGNITY AND RESPONSIBILITY OF EACH INDIVIDUAL

The second foundation of this new society was democracy. This took root from the new realization of the dignity of men and women made in the image of God, to whom they were directly accountable for all they did and said. How could such people allow their consciences to be guided by bishops appointed by a secular prince? And if the congregation chose the minister, why should they not also choose their political ruler? So the growing democracy in the church led on to demands for political democracy, which cut at the power base of kings. As King James I realized and said bluntly, "No bishop, no king." It was the king's refusal thus to meet their requests that drove the Pilgrim fathers to sail the Atlantic and set up their own self-governing churches in New England.

In Europe at the beginning of the seventeenth century, the monarchy and aristocracy still ruled and the lower classes still knew their place. The Puritans in England and Scotland, the Huguenots in France, the Calvinists in Holland, the Protestant cantons in Switzerland, and the Protestant states of Germany, helped by the Swedes, all had to fight for their new faith, and out of these battles democracy gradually emerged. The emigrant community in New England didn't stop until they and their descendants had created the first democracy. Spurred on by the American example, democracy spread until, three centuries on, the West came to be defined by its democratic form of government.

THE SCIENTIFIC METHOD

While the fight went on for political change, another group was setting in motion the scientific breakthrough that was also to transform Western society in the next three centuries. According to Professor Sir Herbert Butterfield, author of *The History of Science,* from whom I learned history at Cambridge, the scientific method emerged from a "shuttle of ideas between Holland and England."

Protestant thinkers in these two nations believed that the Bible, the book of God's words, showed the character of the Creator, and that they should study nature, the book of God's works, with the same humility and respect with which they studied the Bible. Science should be based, not on their own theories, but wholly on what they found, by practical experiment, in nature. So they abandoned Greek metaphysics for experimental science.

Francis Bacon was the thinker of the movement. His thinking stems directly from the nature of God as revealed in the Bible. God the Creator was good, and the world he had given us was for our use, so we should study the "book of God's works" as we had studied the Bible, "the book of God's words."

As we saw in the preface, the Bible taught that there was only one Creator, so the laws of nature must be the same everywhere—orderly, rational, stable, and "for the relief of man's estate"—so it was our duty to apply our new knowledge for the common good.

Working on these Christian foundations, the inventors of the scientific method have transformed the world. Infant deaths are far fewer, there are cures for deadly diseases, and most illnesses can now be prevented; diet is better, life spans have lengthened, and we have a far better understanding of what makes us healthy. Crop yields are much higher, and transport is swifter and safer.

THE NEW PAGANISM

Today we take the work ethic, democracy, and the scientific method for granted, forgetting their origin. But because we have turned our backs on the beliefs that undergird them, all three are very much at risk.

The rise of paganism in Western culture reminds us that we cannot take the Christian basis of the scientific method for granted. Other people believe in many gods, not just one, and see the world as disorderly, irrational, unstable, and malign. These pagan beliefs are now infiltrating the West. They show up most vividly in art, where society wears its heart on its sleeve. As we pass the chaotic art in the airport departure lounge, we may be grateful that the aircraft is still designed by the scientific method.

Because the scientific method has lost its moral base, however, there seems to be no way to limit the harm we can do to nature or to each other. We are burning up fossil fuel at such a rate that the whole climate of the world is in danger of being damaged, and we have made no moral distinction between weapons aimed to destroy an opposing armed force and weapons that cannot avoid destroying millions of innocent civilians, old and young alike.

The Christian work ethic should lead to the creation of wealth not by the destruction of the world's natural resources but by their proper use. Christians believe that the human race holds natural resources in trust from God, and that these resources should not only be passed on to succeeding generations intact but, as in Christ's parables of the pounds and the talents, should be improved in the passing. No generation should leave behind deserts and dustbowls, nor should they leave natural hazards like nuclear waste.

THE RISE OF PROFESSIONALISM

If there is a key institution in the rise of the West, it is the profession. It is the professions that have created the new "knowledge economy." They are the source of old knowledge, the fountain of new knowledge, the passageway between what we know in theory and what we can apply in practice. They are also the court of ethics, protecting the public by setting standards of professional conduct and applying sanctions to those who break the standard. They embody the aims and ideals of innovation for the public good that have taken us so far in the last four hundred years.

Great skill and ingenuity is needed to improve living standards for a rising population, to lift the poor from poverty, and to feed the starving. The weight of poverty is much too heavy to be lifted by simple redistribution. New ways have to be found of both creating and distributing wealth, and this calls for immense dedication and very hard work by the professionals in the world's dynamo economies.

In the eighteenth and nineteenth centuries, the first professionals developed institutions aimed to increase the level of knowledge and competence. One of the first was the British Royal Society, founded to develop the new experimental science. There was a steady rise in educational standards and in the number and quality of universities, which began to teach medicine and science as well as the humanities.

The profession helps each generation learn from those who have gone before, add to that knowledge, and teach it to those who follow them. Professions today achieve ever higher standards of knowledge, and tough examinations guarantee the competence of their members. Professions also try to make sure that the public can trust their members, and they expel anyone who falls below their ethical standards. This reflects the Christian duty to keep the highest standards of honesty and integrity, just as their aim of developing the state of knowledge reflects Christ's parable of the talents.

Running through all professionalism is the overriding objective of service to the community. The nurse and doctor are there to help the sick get well, the teacher to help the children learn, the aeronautical engineer to make sure that planes are safe to fly, the lawyer to see that the client has the best legal advice and protection. Certainly, the professional makes money; but service should come first. It is the dominance of professional standards that distinguishes the countries with a Christian culture. Christian professionals should put some time into the committees of their profession and should fight to see that ethical standards are not undermined.

Professional standards act as a great protection to the Christian when corporate bosses bring pressure to cut corners. If we have to choose between the short-term hazard of losing a job and the long-term hazard of being expelled from our profession, we know—and so should those who employ us know—which choice we must make.

So, new medical knowledge should not be kept as a kind of monopoly to fetch the highest price, but for the service of the whole community. And those who have mastered their subject have a duty to the next generation who, in turn, have to add to that knowledge before they too pass it on. In this way, generation by generation, knowledge has grown. Today the West is a "knowledge society."

The duty of care was also developed as each profession drew up its ethical code and its powers to discipline those members who did not keep to it. Professionalism developed until most disciplines had their own institutions and training. Membership in the profession demanded standards not only of competence but also of professional ethics, with penalties for those who did not keep them.

Professional qualifications are tough, and rightly so. But the business of putting them into practice is tougher still. It is a great help to have a good supervisor as a role model and mentor, someone who will stretch us and give us responsibility, who will pass on the folklore of the profession, which the textbooks miss. We need someone to whom we will listen when they point out our mistakes; above all, we need someone whose example will teach us how to treat clients and colleagues with respect. Good supervisors are hard to find, but well worth the search.

Part of the development of our talents must be an effort, with method and self-discipline, to improve the state of the art. At the frontiers of knowledge and practice we are on our own. And, as that old management guru Peter Drucker said in the quote at the chapter head, we must set our own high standards of what good work should be.

PERSONAL DISCIPLINE

A vital part of the new ethic was trust. The apostles taught the early church not to quarrel with each other and never to go to law against each other. Trust is not just about money; it is about personal relations too. The new breed of merchants knew that they had to get along well together. They knew that Christians must be determined to control their antipathies and refuse to let other people get under their skin, to ride all personal misunderstandings lightly and refuse to be offended. Anger feeds on itself, and if we discipline ourselves instead, we will find a good deal more energy left for the job.

The quarrels and duels of the aristocracy were a self-indulgence that had no place in the life of the new generation of hardworking merchants and bankers. Self-discipline created trust, and trust turned the wheels of business. The new generation was, above all, serious. It was the contrast, at another level, between the dashing but undisciplined cavalry of Prince Rupert fighting for King Charles I and the solid strength of Cromwell's New Model Army, which won the English Civil War. "Pray to God," Cromwell told them, "and keep your powder dry." That painstaking detail was the difference between defeat and victory.

It was the same tough attention to detail by which dedicated engineers worked to give us the new inventions of the industrial age, from the steam engine to internal combustion. They wanted to change the world, and patiently and with infinite pains they did. And yet this toughness has its own excitement, which a frivolous life can never give.

Nothing is a greater source of strength than a sense of competence, a feeling that you are on top of the situation and that you have the initiative. You can not only ride out the storms but have a sense of exhilaration in doing it. If we have allowed the job to get on top of us, we should look again at our priorities and the way we organize our work. If we tackle the tough problems first, the rest will usually look after themselves. And, as we go up the hierarchy, we need to learn how to delegate, so that we will have time for the problems no one else can handle.

The person with a trained and disciplined mind will have the versatility to examine and assess new evidence and then think the problem through. His self-assurance in a crisis and under the pressure of people and events will not be based on prejudice but on knowledge. We are not all born with good judgment, but most of us can pick it up with experience.

Christ has taught us the duty to serve others before ourselves; so we should set higher and tougher standards than those set for us, and should look more closely and critically at our performance. The Christian should be a self-starter who does not need to be pushed; the one who goes for the tough problem and breaks it; the one who, when a critical decision has to be made, has done his homework.

As soon as we are given responsibility, we run into problems that no one else is going to solve for us. We reach for the textbook; but textbooks have a way of skipping around corners, so we should also listen to the veterans who, sometime in a long life, have been around those corners before. They may not be as lucid; they may have acted by instinct and may not be able to articulate their reasons. But we ignore their instinct at our peril.

LEARNING NEVER STOPS

The veterans we work with have learned over the years why one process works and another does not. The veteran salesman knows the market. The veteran teacher knows how to grip the imagination of the young. The veteran boss of a construction site knows how to pick good workers who will do the job on time. The young professional who wants to make big changes, all with their own compelling logic, should listen to these old hands first to find the vital factor which their own logic has so far left out.

As young doctors follow the old ones on hospital rounds, they pick up the skills of diagnosis and the trial and error that narrows the possibilities until they all point in one direction. And, even then, they learn to check again, in case they were wrong.

A management consultant asked whether the hospital computer, fed with the patient's symptoms, gave a more reliable diagnosis than the doctor's. His most interesting finding was not on the computer's performance; it was that the success record of the most brilliant doctors was not so good as those in the second rank, who always took the trouble to check again! If I have learned anything in a working life, it is the need to stop and check again.

Just as hospital doctors need to do the ward rounds to see their patients for themselves, so, whatever job we do, we need to get out to see what is going on. However many reports you get, you always learn something new and vital by going to look. The figures in the monthly reports tell you what has happened; but unless you visit, they do not tell you why. A bad atmosphere comes through very quickly, and the responses to questions show at once whether people are on top of the job.

HOW HARD SHOULD WE WORK?

Today we seem to have lost any sense of rhythm in our work, but getting the right pace is the key to steady performance. Exhausted people make bad decisions. Rowing at Cambridge taught me the discipline of rhythm. I can still hear our coach: "Don't rush. Swing easy forward and then HARD through the water! Easy forward and HARD back." An effective crew does not look rushed, and effective professionals should be sure that, physically and mentally, their rhythm of work keeps them on top of the job.

From listening to those trapped in it, I doubt the need for most of this frenetic activity. There are clients we can do without. The best law firms, consultants, and accountants are those who turn down business so that they can give quality time and wise advice. Rather than working overtime, we should devote more time, if we can, to giving our problems some solid logical thought.

We should also remember that a wife has only one husband, a husband only one wife, and that both need time with each other. If we have children, they need time with both father and mother, and they need us there whenever there is a crisis in their small lives—not just in the narrow range of "quality time," as if they were just another client or customer who could only be given half an hour at most. We should never, fathers or mothers, see children as a problem to be solved. They are people, the gift of a good God.

He has given us the instinct to look after them, and to them he has given the instinct to depend on us.

UNEMPLOYMENT

At the other extreme to the overworked professional are those who want to work but cannot find a job. Can they help themselves? Can the government help them? Can the church do anything for them? We seem to live in a society full of opportunity where there ought to be jobs for the finding. It's easy to believe that, for those out of work, it is their own fault; and also to believe that, if they did not have government handouts, they would be forced to find work.

The downside of a fast-moving, competitive economy, which rewards those in work with higher and higher incomes, is that progress in some industries and some areas means decline in other industries and other regions. The "rust belt" goes into decline and "high tech" takes over. But pity the people trained all their life in the old industries.

The first duty of the state is to keep the economy on the move. That way, those out of work have more chance of getting another job of one sort or another. Or, if a husband cannot get a job quickly, maybe his wife, son, or daughter can. If the growth keeps on, they can all move to a city where there are more jobs.

The Anglo-Saxon economies currently tend to go for growth. The "Rhine model" has, until now, put more emphasis on protecting those in work. It makes change more difficult, or imposes expensive conditions for layoffs. The limitation of the Anglo-Saxon model is that growth so easily turns into growth of imports and huge trading deficits. High growth, in an economy as big as America's, can also carry an unacceptable cost to nonrenewable resources such as oil. But for the same reason, high growth in the industrial democracies should also help poorer countries, which rely on the demand for their primary products. So governments are reluctant to slow down the great industrial machine unless the reasons are very compelling, and the Anglo-Saxon countries feel that if the "Rhine model" lifted some of its labor-protection, their rate of unemployment could come down to the American level.

In a European study of the American economy, we found that new investment tended to go to the areas where there was enough spare labor, and if the labor was unskilled, then the initial investments would be for cheaper unskilled labor; but over time, the skills would grow and attract higher-quality investment. So, over ten or twenty years, there was a corrective market mechanism at work. Meanwhile, with a single language, American labor seemed to be more mobile than European labor.

But for Christians, these economic mechanisms are not enough. We believe that men and women were not made to be idle but to be active and creative like God, in whose image we were made. In Israel, the laws of Moses decreed that the land, which was their means of living, should not be alienated from the family. In the fiftieth year, the year of Jubilee, any land that had been transferred had to go back to the original family.

Today, life is not so simple. Access to work is mainly through organizations. Where the organizations flourish, there are jobs; where they fail, there is unemployment. So it is the duty of governments, both federal and state, to do what they can to see that there is work for all. It would be a lot easier to solve the problem of how this is done if full employment were a first priority in every civilized society.

For four decades, full employment was central to all economic policy in most European democracies. And for four decades it worked well. The key to it was a close engagement between government and industry, so that government policy could be geared to the optimum performance of industry. It was easier for government and industry to understand each other without such formal arrangements in smaller countries like Holland, Denmark, and Sweden. France had the Commissariat General du Plan, and Germany had well-funded chambers of commerce. Britain started a planning process after the war when resources were extremely scarce, dropped it in the fifties, but reinvented it in the sixties.

In Britain, the result was four decades of full employment. The downside was that the rate of demand needed to keep employment high put the pressure on the labor market, which encouraged inflationary wage awards and a low but steady rate of inflation. So the debate between government, trade unions, and industry was on how to get out of this wage-price spiral. But at no point until the 1980s was there any question of abandoning the policy of full employment.

Both Britain and the new European Common Market also had policies of high government investment in health, education, and infrastructure such as freeways, and all of us had to balance our national budgets with limited natural resources. The only way of finding the money was a higher level of taxes than any of us have now, but, despite that, full employment was woven into the mix of policies. Because France's President de Gaulle twice vetoed our membership in the Common Market, Britain did not enjoy the tariff-free market of its main competitors. The issue was how, without their higher cash-flow from tariff-free trade, business could find the funds to invest in the new products that would give us export-led growth. The other issue was how to prevent wage inflation.

In Britain, the focus of these debates was the National Economic Development Council (NEDC), on which I served for seven years, five as director general. My main contribution was to set up mini-councils for each major industry, where government officials sat with the industry leaders and the leaders of the main labor unions. Their input gave us a far more down-to-earth feel for the needs of industry and of government polices which would help them. The NEDC met monthly, chaired by either the prime minister or the chancellor, flanked by the major economic ministers. There were eight leaders of industry and six from the labor unions.

The debates were lively and well publicized. Just as open democratic government helps political decision making, so the councilors across the round council table all made an impact on each other. Foolish ideas were cut down to size and good ones got the attention they needed. The results were good, too. In my seven years on the Council, the rate of industrial investment rose steadily and a substantial trade deficit was turned into a surplus (even though we were still outside the Common Market), and there was full employment.

These good results did not survive the second oil shock in 1979, when the rate of unemployment doubled and Britain abandoned the policy of full employment. Full employment seemed to involve too much wage restraint and too much taxation. From then on, the rich got very much richer and the poor poorer.

The Roosevelt memorial in Washington has a line of unemployed men waiting hopelessly and an inscription with Roosevelt's justification for spending federal money to get people back to work. Christians have an even stronger justification. God put into men and women, made in his image, his own creative instinct. He gave both Adam and Eve work to do, and that went on "by the sweat of your brow" after the Fall (Gen. 3:19). So we all have this sense that our life should have some meaning and purpose. For the last seven years it has been my job to encourage churches in their active help for those whom society has put on the margins, and I have been in city districts with an unemployment rate among the young of 40 percent. Their overwhelming feeling is lack of purpose—nothing seems worth doing. If the jobs were there, they could see some hope, but jobs are not there, and there are older and more skilled people out of work too.

Christians, at least, ought to insist that government's first priority in the management of the economy should be full employment.

2

WEALTH

"The love of money is a root of all kinds of evil."
THE APOSTLE PAUL (1 TIM. 6:10)

*"Store up for yourselves treasures in heaven. . . . For where
your treasure is, there your heart will be also."*
JESUS CHRIST (MATT. 6:20-21)

*"I have heard confessions to every kind of
sin—except covetousness."*
A CATHOLIC PRIEST

About an hour's drive out of Washington, on the way to the Blue
Ridge, you come to hunting country, with stone walls and rolling
fields. One weekend we went on a church fundraising "stable
tour" to the Mellon stables, the largest in the area. Except for one
stable, they were empty. It had been Paul Mellon's enthusiasm.
Now he was dead and all the care and skill, all the breeding and
training, all the anxious and thrilling moments at the races were
just history.

The one remaining horse was the hunter owned and ridden by
the late Jackie Onassis. She had gone, but her favorite horse lived

on, looking out at us over the half-door. Jackie had been the daughter of a millionaire, wife and widow of a president of the United States, and then wife and widow of a billionaire Greek ship owner. Now she too was just history.

At least Paul Mellon and Jackie Onassis had enjoyed life in their own way. But not "the richest man in the world," sitting at the next table at a lunch in London's Savoy Hotel. I have never seen anyone who looked so unhappy as the late J. Paul Getty, his face etched in misery. He was the living antidote to any desire to be a billionaire.

Still, we would all like to be just a little richer than we are. It is very hard, even in a society that is richer than any in human history, to be totally content with what we have.

But we would not be where we are today if the founding fathers of the Western world had not made a clean break with the high spending habits of the society into which they had been born. It was not just the Pilgrim fathers, who gave up the riches of Europe for the barren shores of North America. The hardworking Huguenots in France despised the chateaux of the French aristocracy. While Louis XIV built the extravagant palace of Versailles, they plowed their profits into factories and inventory. The Dutch and English invested their money in merchant ships and into the equipment needed to make the products of the new science.

Religion and the Rise of Capitalism

Religion did not produce capitalism, which has been with us since the beginning of history. But it did produce the savings without which the industrial revolution could never have taken place. Not for this new, hard-working generation the ruffs and feathers of the land-owning nobility, the great houses on huge estates. They had few servants, plain carriages, modest clothes, and modest houses. They did not fight duels or gamble; but they changed the world.

For a long time, the two cultures lived side by side—Puritan New England and the slave-based estates of Tidewater Virginia; but after the War of Independence, and especially after the Civil War, the old style went into decline in America and, with the rise of industry and commerce in Protestant Europe, it went into decline there too.

But riches corrupt. Today both Britain and the United States are spending far more than they are earning. In the last two decades of the old millennium, and now moving into the new millennium, both countries have huge trading deficits, and these cannot go on forever. And within both countries the rich get richer and the poor get poorer. Somehow more money does not make us more generous.

There are rich people in the Bible. Job, Abraham, Isaac, and Jacob were all rich. So, later, was Solomon. The Bible teaches that it is not the amount of our wealth that matters but the way we get it, how we use it, and our ability to sit lightly to it. Paul explains (1 Tim. 6:6-9, RSV),

> There is great gain in godliness with contentment; for we brought nothing into the world, and we cannot take anything out of the world; but if we have food and clothing, with these we shall be content. But those who desire to be rich will fall into temptation, into a snare, into many senseless and hurtful desires that plunge men into ruin and destruction.

Again Paul says to Timothy (vv. 17-18),

> As for the rich in this world, charge them not to be haughty, nor to set their hopes on uncertain riches but on God who richly furnishes us with everything to enjoy. They are to do good, to be rich in good deeds, liberal and generous.

Practicing Christians are likely to be richer than their neighbors. We are taught to work harder, be more trustworthy and responsible, and develop our talents to the full; we are not to gamble or waste our money on conspicuous consumption—it would be odd if all this did not put us ahead. And looking around the world, the Western democracies, rooted in this ethic, all have personal incomes far greater than anywhere else. If those with the skill overspend, leaving no capital to invest, then the rest of the world will suffer. The West is the dynamo of the world economy, and we have no right to squander all the wealth on ourselves.

The rich should not get richer by making the poor poorer.

"You shall not steal" is one of the Ten Commandments, and the Law of Moses also prohibits usury (see Ex. 22:25). The prophet Jeremiah warns against exploitation of the poor:

> Woe to him who builds his house by unrighteousness, and his upper rooms by injustice; who makes his neighbor serve him for nothing, and does not give him his wages (22:13, RSV).

James condemns those who use their riches to oppress the poor and those who keep back the wages of their laborers (2:6; 5:4).

We may swear that we don't break any of these old commands, and that the laws of the land are against exploitation. But it is we who make the laws. We are all citizens with a vote; and, in most Western countries today, the rich majority outvote the poor minority. The majority now have houses or apartments with all the latest gadgets; they have automobiles, jobs, regular vacations, and money left over for smart clothes, entertainment, and eating out. Most of that majority have savings and investments in the stock market. And their votes decide the policies of government.

President Reagan's reduction of income taxes won him a second term and George Bush was elected president in 1988 on his promise, "Read my lips: no new taxes." When Bill Clinton first came to office, I listened to an enthusiastic Senator John Rockefeller outlining the proposed new health policy, aimed to help those who did not have private health insurance. But it would have needed taxpayer money, so it was dropped.

If taxes can't be raised to keep inflation and imports under control, then government depends on interest rates alone, pushing them higher just when new investment is needed to meet rising demand. Though U.S. interest rates have come down at the time of writing, U.S. dollar corporate bonds cost 6.89 percent against euro corporate bonds at 5.83 percent (*The Economist*, May 3, 2002), a cash layout of 18 percent extra for a new job-creating investment in the United States. This means job losses in the United States and the spiraling trade deficit which we have considered.

The higher interest rates also benefit those who have money and hurt those who need loans. On that alone, the rich get richer and the poor get poorer, as we the electorate have willed. Those who cannot afford private medical insurance still have to wait at the end of the line.

This "monetarism" (reliance on interest rates alone to guide the economy) has another side effect, which has damaged both Britain and America. Higher interest rates attract an inflow of capital, which has made both the dollar and the pound overvalued against other currencies. That overvaluation has damaged our export industries, made foreign imports more competitive, and given us huge foreign trade deficits. The eighties and nineties turned America from the largest creditor nation in the world into its largest debtor. Both Britain and America still run huge overseas trade deficits.

By contrast, the "Rhine model" countries of the European

Union have higher taxes and lower interest rates—and a foreign trading surplus.

WORKER PROTECTION

Labor laws in the Rhine model are much more protective of employees than in the Anglo-Saxon model. It is harder to fire workers, and the cost of hiring them is increased by payments for pension and sickness. In some countries, such as Germany and Holland, trade unions also have to be consulted before management makes any major decision, such as a merger, that might affect jobs.

The monetarists say that European business needs much more flexible labor markets in order to compete. But the ultimate measure of competition is the foreign trade balance, and the Rhine model countries have a foreign trade surplus compared with the huge trade deficits of America and the United Kingdom. Trade surpluses can go on forever, but sooner or later trade deficits put countries into the hands of their creditors.

More important than this worldly wisdom, the Bible teaches clearly that the strong must look after the weak. The Old Testament prophets tell employers that they must not exploit their workers. America was not built on highly regulated labor markets, nor was industrial Britain. But unregulated markets had their price. In 1909 my Uncle Fred was killed in his twenties by faulty electrical equipment in a Rockefeller mine in Idaho. Throughout the period of decisive growth in the nineteenth century, Christian leaders campaigned for laws that would make employers look after their workers. England's great nineteenth-century Christian reformer Lord Shaftesbury spent his life in promoting legislation to protect workers from greedy employers, and he is honored to this day by an avenue named after him in the heart of London's West End.

Certainly, corporations have to compete. I've spent twelve years as a CEO and I know that competition can lead to plant closure and putting people out of work. But where a loss-making plant has to be closed, management should look after the workers who lose a hundred percent of their income on the day the doors shut. Christians should not object to regulations that make management consult the workers beforehand and compensate them for their loss afterwards.

In my experience, a partnership between management and labor, where people trust each other and are making a common effort, is far more successful financially than the cold money-making machine. If we look after our workers, they will look after us. If we do not, they will do what they have to and no more. The one will warn us about problems ahead, the others will not bother; the one will find better ways of doing the job, the others will do the job like automatons and have their minds elsewhere.

Usury

As we have seen, in the parables of the talents and the pounds (Matthew 25 and Luke 19), Jesus commends servants who earned interest on the money their master had left with them. He would not have commended the act, even in a parable, if investing money at interest were wrong. The usury prohibited in the Law of Moses was the charging of excessive interest, amounts that could only be paid back out of capital. Charging interest at a rate that can be paid out of profits is not exploitation; it is part of the helpful process of putting savings to work.

But there are still moneylenders today who exploit the poor. In you are living on the margin and spending every cent every week on necessities, what do you do if the stove breaks down? Meals out are more expensive, and you hope that you may get a new job soon, so you borrow from the finance company at 200 percent or more. When you can't repay the loan, the finance company suggests that you just borrow the amount of the extra interest. So you take that easy option until you find that, with accumulated interest, the debt is out of control. Some churches now have "debt centers" where unpayable debts can be added up, an estimate made of basic personal or family needs, and a proposal put to the lender, who usually finds it cheaper to settle for that than to go to court. Churches also organize local savings funds, which can help those in need at low interest rates.

How Should We Use Our Money?

How should we use the money God has given us? Let's start where most Christians would agree. Gambling is a fool's game, motivated by pure greed. The odds are heavily against the gambler. I once sat next to a bookmaker's wife at a wedding. I asked her what horses she backed. She said, "My old man doesn't allow me to bet. He asks, 'Who do you think keeps you in fur coats?'"

But we can also gamble with our investments. There are people who have money and to spare, who review their whole investment portfolio every day. They may argue that they are only doing the same as farmers, who go out every day to look at their crops. But the farmer has to be able to spot trouble fast and put right what has gone wrong. There is a difference between looking after our capital by putting it in reliable stocks and the greedy insistence on quick capital gains, which makes us obsessed with the daily movement of the markets.

We should, of course, invest our money intelligently, where it will do the most long-term good; and, since life is unpredictable, we should spread the risk and maybe once a quarter we should review it with our broker. But the rest of the time we should forget about it.

Investors' obsession with short-term movements has put corporate management today under incessant pressure to produce a steady quarter-by-quarter increase in its share price. Management knows that if it does not do this, then it is vulnerable to hostile takeover.

But corporations must make new investment in the research, development, and hardware needed for new competitive products. This takes several years to pay off, and meanwhile the interest on the investment depresses the corporate profits and the share price. The easy alternative is to boost short-term profits and the share price by taking over companies with a lower ratio of share price to profits. Another alternative is to boost profits by massive downsizing. Both of these alternatives can have high long-term costs, as does the neglect of long-term investment. But corporate management can be tempted to "go with the flow" and award itself "golden parachutes" so that, when the long-term damage shows up, they will be safely out. That is about as far as you could get from the principles of the generations whose savings and investment built up our nations' wealth!

What drives greed is covetousness, a breach of the tenth commandment. Just because someone else has something, we want it ourselves. It may be the latest fashion, a sleeker automobile, a home in a smarter suburb, a ticket in first class, the latest in electronic equipment, a vacation abroad, a stretch limousine to the theater, or membership in a first-class tennis or golf club. And these are the more moderate, respectable wants.

Most family quarrels are about money—about who gets what when the old folks die. Or, longer lasting, why did my brother, my sister get more than I did? We may talk about the pros and cons of euthanasia, putting the old and ill out of their suffering; but politicians should beware of putting the power of euthanasia into the hands of those who itch to get their hands on the old folks' money!

In its way, covetousness is the natural logic of an age without religious faith. If this is the only world there is, then we should grab what we can, while we can, however we can, and hold onto it hard. But Christians believe that this is a brief, passing life during which we can and must lay up our treasure in heaven. That belief is what drove the apostle Paul through shipwreck, prison, beatings, and ferocious opposition. We are not all called to suffer as he did; but we are told to be content with what we have. And if we have more than we need, we must use it carefully.

CHRISTIAN GIVING

One simple test of a Christian's trust in God is our attitude toward tithing. We cannot dismiss tithing, as many of us do, as a redundant part of the Mosaic Law. Long before Moses, Abraham tithed his gains to Melchizedek, and we are told in the New Testament that Jesus was a High Priest "after the order of Melchizedek." So if it was right for Abraham to tithe to Melchizedek, it is surely right for Christians to give a tenth of our income to Christ. It is true that when Paul tells the Corinthians to set aside weekly a regular part of their wages, he does not mention the tithe which Moses had commanded. But why should Paul expect less than the full tithe? In this as in everything else, Christians are meant to go beyond the letter of the law.

And where is our faith? The Lord, we are told, rewards a cheerful giver. R. T. Kendall, the recently retired American minister of Westminster Chapel, London, argues that the Lord makes sure that no one is ever worse off for tithing. He says, "You cannot out-give God. You'll always find that the 90 percent goes farther." I wouldn't like to be so precise, but experience seems to bear him out. Look at it this way: if our income goes up, God's tithe goes up too.

We need to think hard about the causes to which we give. Much giving is selfish or sentimental. I came under far more pressure as a Member of Parliament to help baby seals with soulful eyes than to help children. The wealthiest charity in my electoral district was for the protection of birds.

Church members have the right to a say in how their church is run, and we have a collective duty to make sure that our gifts go to a work of which the church approves; but we have no right to impose narrow conditions on those whose job it is to assess the needs and the balance of giving. As a treasurer of an international student movement, I found that big givers have big hearts and do not make narrow conditions. I was due to meet a lady who was an oil billionaire on a visit to England. A mid-sized automobile drew up outside our Cambridge church, and two pleasant, unassuming middle-aged ladies got out, the billionaire and her friend. After service, we took them to the Graduate Center, and they all happily pushed their plastic trays along the self-service counter. Over lunch, the billionaire said to me, "If you had a whole wad of money, what would you do with it?" I said that I would give it to student work in Eastern Europe. Christian student groups were springing up all over the formerly communist countries, but they badly needed help and teaching. And there was no more effective form of evangelism than one student to another. In due course the "great wad of money" came without strings and kept on coming every year. Her gentle and unassuming manner was a lesson I have never forgotten.

One of the richest Christians in Britain, Sir John Laing, was also a man of simple tastes who could not understand why God had given him so much money. Those who knew him thought that it was because God was sure that he would use the money well. He put most of it into charitable trusts, which took the best advice as to where to place it, and many Christian causes have been extremely grateful to the Laing trusts.

TODAY'S "WIDOWS AND ORPHANS"

The toughest job of all is to raise money for the poor and unemployed in our own country. We give willingly to famine relief, but we feel that if the poor in our own land only tried they could get themselves out of trouble, and that more money will only encourage more idleness. The nineteenth-century novelist Charles Dickens caricatured this view brilliantly in *Oliver Twist*.

It is a view especially tough on children. I've had to visit a lot of poor districts in the last few years, finding out what has gone wrong and how the churches might help to put it right. We asked seventy church-based city projects what had created the problems of those they were trying to help. Two answers stood out stark and clear. One was the breakup of the family and the other was persistent unemployment.

The dogma of today's intellectual leaders is that keeping the family together is a matter of choice, and that there is no absolute right and wrong—except the rightness of their unproven dogma. So families are breaking up at a faster rate than ever. Most deserted young mothers take on a new man, who has no special liking for the noisy kids around the house. So no one loves them. Then, with our market economy ever more open to competition and change, the local closures and cutbacks throw thousands out of work and, when the youth of such areas leave school, no one wants them. So, in a hopeless and hostile world, they take to drugs—and to crime to fund the addiction. The prison population soars, and those who are not caught make the streets unsafe. Where there is still a solid family, they can help each other, even if it means moving away to another city. But no one cares for these unloved kids. The Old Testament prophets condemn the Israel of their time for neglecting the widows and orphans. Today's social experiments have filled our cities with "widows and orphans," and it is our biblical duty to look after them. It is a tough job, but in most of our cities there are church-based projects doing just that. We need to support them.

The prophets also condemn Israel for failing to look after the aliens, who have no local backup in time of trouble. Most immigrants head for a city where they can find some of their own community, but there are also aliens who are isolated and lonely. Overseas graduate students doing doctorates bring their wives with them, and if the men are busy enough, the wives, especially those who do not speak English, are totally isolated. In Cambridge the churches have set up a hostel for postgraduates that has created a real community and has transformed the lives of the students' wives.

These students are privileged, however, compared with the poor immigrants, who have a much tougher time. Those who look after them earn their undying gratitude. The Democratic Party machine in New York was built up on its care for immigrants. Maybe we in the churches should learn something from the worldly wisdom of the politicians.

CHRISTIAN LOVE IN ACTION

Our Lord showed practical love. He not only taught, but because God is love, he healed the sick and fed the hungry. He met a widow coming out of the city of Nain behind the corpse of her only son. In a day when a woman depended on the help of her male family members, she had lost both of her men. Jesus' love went out to her and he restored her son to life. And if we have the Spirit of God, we should have the same kind of love.

The apostle Paul was the greatest evangelist, but he had this same love. None of the people who went with Paul the prisoner on the boat bound for Rome were in the least deserving. The captain was careless, the passengers were probably all criminals, the sailors tried to abandon the ship, and the soldiers wanted to kill the prisoners. Yet Paul, on his native coast, had warned about the weather; he prayed to God for their safety in the awful gale; and, when God answered, he encouraged the crew to get back to their posts. It was Paul who told them all to have enough to eat to make sure that they had the strength to get to shore; Paul who became aware that the sailors were about to abandon them; and, once on shore, we find the great Apostle to the Gentiles busy gathering sticks for a fire to dry everyone out. If Paul could spend time and energy on the undeserving, who are we to judge them unworthy of our practical help?

The Roman Empire was not converted by lobbying the emperor or by great evangelistic crusades. Pagan superstitions and Greek philosophy were overcome by simple neighborly love. And, as we have seen, when Rome was overthrown, it was love that won over the invading pagan tribes. So we should make sure that we give funds to those who are out there looking after the fatherless children, helping them to come off drugs and to learn how to earn a living—not to mention all the others in trouble, the single mothers, the battered wives, those dying of AIDS, the prisoners and ex-prisoners, and the unemployed. We may not have the gifts to tackle these problems ourselves; but if we tithe, we have the money to show Christian love by helping those who do.

Nor should we forget that, one day, we will all be judged. In the parable of the sheep and the goats, both professed to be Christians. They were divided one from the other on the demonstration of their faith and love for God in their practical concern for those in need. "Whatever you did for one of the least of these brothers of mine, you did for me. . . . whatever you did not do for one of the least of these, you did not do for me" (Matt. 25:40, 45).

THOSE WHO BUILT THE WEST LIVED WELL WITHIN THEIR INCOMES

We need to check back to see where all our Western wealth came from. We've looked at the dynamic breakthrough of the seventeenth-century scientific method, driven on by the new work ethic. But had they followed the extravagant expenditure of the old rich, who lived up to and beyond their incomes, nothing would have been left to come down to us. Louis XIV of France wasted the new wealth of the French Huguenots in years of fruitless war. The rulers of the independent German states each built his extravagant Schloss. The ruling classes of England built the great mansions, now open to the public, with portraits of their self-satisfied, pink-faced owners smiling down at us from under their curly white wigs.

But the builders of the modest homes of the merchants in Amsterdam and London, Boston and Philadelphia, many still standing, saved their profits and reinvested them.

That classic work *Religion and the Rise of Capitalism,* by R. H. Tawney, argues that it was the *religion* of the merchant class that made them create new capital instead of spending their profits. That sharp rise in working capital built the great expansion of trade that has made us rich today. The initial expansion was tough, as the Pilgrim fathers found. But a good part of the surplus went into development, making each year's surplus greater than the last.

So the east coast of America was developed, then the hinterland, then the thirteen colonies became the United States and the investment in farms and forestry rolled over the mountains and into the central plain until the land was full, coast to coast, of hardworking men and women, saving the capital for the railroads and the new industries that made America independent of Europe. And then, in the twentieth century, America went into the lead, with the biggest accumulation of capital in the world. But today the net savings of the nation available for business investment are almost down to zero.

MONEY BRINGS POWER

The Old Testament prophets attacked the power of those who used their money to pervert justice and to oppress the poor. Democracies today try to make sure that money cannot pervert justice. In the nineteenth century, the salaries of British judges were fixed high enough to discourage bribery. In the United States, popular election allows voters to throw out a corrupt judge.

Until the spread of democracy to all levels of society in nine-teenth-century Britain, most of the seats in the elected House of Commons were in the hands of the rich. Now there is a strict limit on individual election expenses; but the rich can still bankroll political parties, as they can in most democracies.

In America, parties and individual candidates have always had to raise funds; but the cost of television time has greatly raised the stakes. A young congressman and I swapped our experiences on fund-raising. I said that we usually spent well under our legal limit, which was $40,000. He said he spent half a million if lucky and a million if not so lucky. I asked him how he raised that amount. He said simply, "Business wants access and we want dollars, so we do a trade." And in fund-raising, the incumbent has a credibility that the challenger lacks, so the smart money goes to the sitting congressmen and senators.

But should money give more access to one voter than to another? Maybe it doesn't. Voters call the offices of their elected members right through the day. With elections every two years to the U.S. House, the Congress is probably closer to its voters than in any other democracy. And the buildings up on the Hill are open to anyone to walk in. But we have to ask whether business would give the money if it did not assume that it gains some priority over

the ordinary voter. Bosses tell employees that they have to contribute to political campaigns because their jobs may depend on it.
Lobbyists for big business have a heavy presence on the Hill, and
their lawyers keep a sharp eye on the texts of proposed legislation.

On many issues there is no conflict between the lobby and the
voter. The interest of the majority of voters in a state or district is
the same as that of its major industries. It is a matter of course that
the congressman for Seattle will look after the aircraft industry; for
Detroit, the automobile industry; for Akron, the tire industry. But
commercial and electoral interests are in conflict on all kinds of
issues, and in a democracy it is the millions of people, not the millions of dollars, that should matter.

In the presidential primaries, only the very rich can provide the
big funds needed; so in 1999 it was the rich donors who decided
that only Gore and Bush would go forward to their respective conventions in 2000. The party conventions might have made the
same decision, but we will never know, because big money made
the decision for them and, as we argue in chapter 4, that power is
a corruption of democracy.

Bribery and Corruption

We do not have to look far to see what has happened in countries
where money has already corrupted the democratic process.
Money talks loud and clear and on a massive scale. The market
becomes warped, uncertainty reduces business to a snail's pace,
and the payoffs divert the capital of the country from productive
use to the maintenance of a small group of family and cronies in
closely guarded luxury. No junta lasts long. Change of government
is by violent coup d'etat, and the ruler's family and cronies are
lucky if they are not caught by their own corruption. President
Peron of Argentina left the Casa Rosada for the safety of a loyal
warship in the River Plate and then called out the tanks. These had

only moved a few hundred yards from the barracks when their bearings seized because Peron, in an excess of greed, had sold off the army's oil!

Corruption is the main single reason why income per capita in most countries is only a tenth of that in the industrial democracies. Corruption is a fungus that grips and holds back economic development while those in power argue about the division of the bribes. In one Caribbean country, a major port was never built because, so it was said, each member of the government wanted to be minister of marine when the contract had to be signed.

None of the industrial democracies has crossed the threshold into corruption. The Italian Christian Democrats came nearest, but the electorate threw them out in time and the party no longer exists. But corruption is an insidious process and we need to make sure that we spot it and stop it in time.

A corrupt society, where no one trusts anyone else, is doomed to poverty. But a society where millions can trust their savings to people they have never met will have the funds to invest in the future. And traders who trust each other and do not have to have the lawyers crawl over every transaction can do far more business and expand far faster. It was the sober, trustworthy merchants of Amsterdam, London, Boston, and New Amsterdam (as New York was then called) who gave international trade its initial boost to levels never dreamed of before.

That is why the bazaar merchants, who exploited every transaction for all they could get out of it, gave way to low-margin/high-volume business between merchants who trusted each other. And as the new banks gained the trust of depositors, interest rates came down and investment went up. But today's society is back to the insistence on maximum short-term gains regardless of the future. The Christian has to stand like a rock against that tide.

3

GOVERNMENT

"The authorities that exist have been established by God."
THE APOSTLE PAUL (ROM. 13:1)

"The business of America is business."
CALVIN COOLIDGE

THE SEPARATE ROLES OF CHURCH AND STATE

The founding fathers of the United States are much revered, but business has for a long time had higher prestige in America than politics. What happens on Wall Street seems far more important than the arguments in caucuses on Capitol Hill.

Yet both of the great apostles, Peter and Paul, tell us that governments are put there by God for our good, and that we must obey them (Rom. 13:1-6 and 1 Pet. 2:11-12). In their day, the power was neither, in Lincoln's words, "by the people" nor "of the people." The Roman emperor was an autocrat whose governor in Jerusalem had condemned Christ to death and whose imperial successors persecuted the Christian church for refusing to worship them.

Rome might have been a pagan power, but, since the state as well as the church was God-given, Christians were to obey its laws—so long as those laws did not conflict with the law of God. Church and state are, in God's order, quite separate. Even in the state of Israel in Old Testament times, each had its own function, its own officers, its own laws, and its own penalties. Aaron was the priest and Moses was, for forty years, the judge who applied the civil law. Under the kings, there was the same separation.

THE DIFFERENCE BETWEEN THE MORAL AND THE CIVIL LAW

The church deals with the God-given moral law of absolute right and wrong. But in applying the civil law, the state has to take into account the sinfulness of human nature. When a woman taken in adultery, "in the very act," was brought before Christ (John 8:3-11, KJV), he was asked whether, as the law of Moses said, she should be stoned. Jesus condemned the adultery as sin; but it is clear that the civil punishment by stoning had long fallen into disuse, otherwise there would have been no point in their question. Though she had been taken "in the very act," they had not brought along the offending man as well, so they were not interested in justice but in embarrassing Jesus. He called their bluff by suggesting that whoever was innocent should throw the first stone; and, starting with the oldest, they all crept away. The moral law is eternal, but the civil punishment is for the government to decide.

Telling lies is morally wrong, but the law today only imposes a penalty when lies can be shown to do material harm to someone else. We Christians are entitled to the view that, unless the life of the mother is physically at risk, to take the life of an unborn baby is wrong; and we are right to be appalled by this massacre of the innocents. But if we fail to persuade the majority of the voters to accept our view, the government will not prosecute women who are determined to have an abortion anyway. The government will hesitate to impose any new law if it is unsure whether it can be enforced. It is up to the churches to change hearts and minds. That is the battle that has been fought before all great reforms have been made into law.

In any direct conflict between his duty to God and his duty to the state, the Christian's duty to God must, of course, come first. When the Sanhedrin told the apostles not to preach, Peter refused to stop preaching. He had to obey God, not men. But where no such conflict is involved, we must obey the government God has set over us, democratic or not.

In countries where Christianity has been the predominant religion, there has normally been a working partnership between church and state. The civil law is based on Christian teaching of right and wrong, and the Christian church has taught our duty to the state as well as to our own families and our neighbors. Where there is widespread church attendance, the moral law is generally respected and most disputes between neighbors are settled without litigation.

Every society needs a code of right and wrong that also recognizes which kinds of behavior are socially acceptable and which are unacceptable. Such a consensus makes life safer, more predictable, and more manageable. Take away codes of self-restraint and we put an impossible burden on the police.

THE MELTDOWN OF THE MORAL ORDER

All religions depend on some organized body—church, mosque, or temple—for their moral laws, and all have supported the institution of the family as the place where rules of behavior are taught to the young. Communism outlawed religion but found that it had to substitute its own ferociously strict moral order, enforced by a police state and an army of informers. Only in the last forty years has the Christian moral order been repudiated by traditionally Christian states. The repudiation of its moral order is a dangerous and unprecedented experiment—never attempted by any state or society. Only communism has been so arrogant as to destroy the social order on this scale, and no one wants the tyranny which that experiment brought.

Our own Western social order is now nearing meltdown. The law cannot possibly deal with every quarrel. Nor can the new codes of "politically correct" behavior, because they are drawn up by the intellectual elite and do not come from the heart of society. Sexual harassment, for instance, used to be discouraged by powerful social sanctions. Now it is encouraged by the rapid growth of pornography, which removes the dignity of women and treats them as no more than sex objects. How can the cumbersome force of the law deal with that massively promoted degeneration in relations between the sexes?

The most damaging result of the attacks on the Christian moral and social order has been the widespread breakup of the family, which is the most basic and most effective social organization in all religions and societies in all ages. There is no tried and tested substitute for that combination of love and discipline, where we learn early on how to relate to other people and where we discover what is tolerable behavior and what is not. Neither social science nor the law can repair the awful damage of the family's decline. Teachers know at once which children come from broken families, which boys will get into trouble, and which girls will soon be single mothers. But teachers are no substitute for a family.

Religion, whose moral law helps to hold together not only families but whole societies, is now rubbished and sidelined. In countries where Christianity is the leading religion, we are told that it is intolerant to believe that any one religion is right. Our new secular high priests pose as guardians of the minority religions and imply that if Christians had their way, we would be intolerant of every other religion. They could not be more wrong. Minority religions know who their friends are, and they stand together with Christians against the destruction of the moral order.

The Christian faith teaches racial tolerance. As the apostle John repeats four times in the last book of the Bible, Christians are from "every nation, tribe, people and language" (Rev. 7:9). So racial discrimination is wrong. And, because Christianity has now spread across all nations and peoples, it is a minority religion in most countries, where it must make the case for religious tolerance and ask for constitutional protection. Turkey, for instance, is a mainly Islamic country, but the tiny Christian minority are protected because modern Turkey is a secular state and Turkish governments—and the army, which sees itself as the guardian of the constitution—very much want to keep it that way. Kazakhstan, a traditionally Muslim country with a Russian Orthodox minority, now recognizes the growing Protestant churches too.

The largest Christian minority in the world are the Chinese Christians, estimated at between 50 and 90 million. The Indian church also needs the protection of India's secular constitution against the militants of other religions. Christians in countries like Russia and Greece need protection against the dominance of one national church. So Christians do not need lectures on the benefits of secular constitutions that guarantee freedom to all religions.

GOVERNMENTS CANNOT IMPOSE MORALITY

Intolerance in the West comes not from religion but from the attempt by today's intellectual leadership to impose their own experimental secular moral order, the rules of "political correctness." But though it dominates the commanding heights of the media, political correctness does not have the same support at the grassroots level, and it has no nationwide organization like the church to argue its message. Therefore, codes of politically correct behavior rely on government enforcement. But if government is the judge of right and wrong, we have a totalitarian state.

There must also be some moral standards against which government itself is judged, as the Old Testament prophets judged the governments of their day and as Christ judged the Jewish leaders of his day. If whatever government says is right, and whatever it condemns is wrong, then we will find that the rules are steadily changed in its favor.

We think it could not happen. So did the Germans in the 1930s. A former colleague of mine, Philip von Bismarck, whose great-grandfather had been the first chancellor of a united Germany, told me, "We did not think that the chancellor of Germany could be a gangster. And by the time we found out, it was too late."

Christians in the Soviet Union suffered under an enforced secular moral order for seventy years. The appalling "apartheid" regime in South Africa was imposed by government despite the protests of Christians in South Africa and around the world. It was only when the Dutch Reformed Church was finally persuaded that the Christian faith prohibited racial barriers that the regime was persuaded to change.

In a country with many faiths, it is not in the interest of any faith to concede to government the right to cross the divide between church and state and impose its own moral order. Governments are subject to the same moral law as the ordinary citizen and are not entitled to call wrong right or right wrong, after the example of the twentieth-century totalitarian governments of Europe, fascist as well as communist.

The politically correct argument is that, in a multi-faith society, no one faith has a right to impose its own moral order on others. But all the major faiths defend the family as the basic social institution and all oppose its breakup. And government, if it wants public support for the law of the land, must take some notice of the predominant faith on which the country's law was founded.

Of course the church itself can be corrupted. But the predominant faith in America, the faith of its founders and of its main immigrant communities, including Africans and Hispanics, has a written record of what is unchangeably right and wrong. Those who are told to love their neighbors as themselves were clearly wrong when they went on a series of crusades against Islam. The Bible told the church in the Middle Ages, as it tells us, "not by might nor by power, but by my Spirit, says the LORD" (Zech. 4:6). So they had no business to appoint bishops as secular rulers, to confuse church and state. That intermingling of spiritual and secular power is the "spirit of antichrist" of which the apostle John speaks in his first letter (4:3). The Dutch Reformed Church did itself no good by being too closely associated with racist governments. In some other African countries today, the church is also in danger of being too closely associated with corrupt regimes.

There are, we know, great differences between Christianity, Islam, Hinduism, Sikhism, Shintoism, Confucianism, and other mainstream religions. But all in their own way try to set out a moral order; and all, without exception, put the family at the center of the moral order. The destruction of the family as the nursery of civil order is a wild experiment, and secular humanism cannot defend it on grounds of religious liberty. Nor can it be argued that scientific integrity compels secular humanists to question Christianity, since, as we have seen above, experimental science is founded on the Bible's revelation about God the Creator (and the search for origins can be no more than the metaphysical speculation that was banished by the founding fathers of modern science!). Secular humanism does not have a leg to stand on, and if we cannot see through its dangerous errors, it will be the death of Western society.

GOVERNMENTS ARE ENTITLED TO DEFEND THEIR COUNTRY AGAINST ITS ENEMIES

The Acts of the Apostles records the conversion of a Roman centurion, but it does not report his resignation from the Roman army. Despite a minority of Christian pacifists, the great majority of Christians down through the ages have believed in the right of a nation to defend itself by force. The apostle Paul told the Romans (chapter 13) that "the governing authorities . . . [do] not bear the sword in vain" (vv. 1, 4, RSV). Roman soldiers rescued Paul from the fury of a Jewish mob. Roman cavalry escorted him to safety in Caesarea. But alongside this acknowledgment of a nation's right to self-defense is the Christian insistence that the war has to be just and should be fought against opposing armed forces and not against innocent civilians.

When King David made the military census needed for a standing army, God's rebuke was swift and drastic (2 Samuel 24). All of David's battles as king of Israel had been defensive, and that was the way God wanted it to remain.

The nuclear weapons that ended World War II in the Pacific did kill the innocent. Our present generation is not responsible for that, but because these bombs have once been used, we must live under the only too credible threat of nuclear war. So we should encourage the efforts and treaties that have taken us such a long way toward nuclear disarmament.

Most Christians agreed that the North Atlantic Treaty Organization (NATO) was justified in keeping its own nuclear weapons as a counter-threat to those of the Soviet Union. So long as there was "mutually assured destruction" ("MAD" was the appropriate acronym), it was believed that neither side would move—and neither did. Finally there was a treaty ("START," the Strategic Arms Reduction Treaty) between the Soviet Union with its Warsaw Pact allies on one side and NATO on the other.

Ironically, of course, the Soviet Union disintegrated within months after the treaty was signed. The danger then, hopefully now remote, was that the Russian government, which took over the Soviet treaties, might lose control of provinces that had nuclear weapons still in place.

Today the main effort in international diplomacy is to discourage the use of nuclear weapons by countries such as India and Pakistan. America's NATO allies fear that the development of an antimissile system by the United States would undo START and make it almost impossible to stop a race by other countries to develop both their nuclear weapons and launching systems. Now that the Soviet threat has gone, it is heavily in the interest of all holders of nuclear weapons to try to reduce their number of weapons by agreement. And the interest of NATO—especially its senior member, the United States—is to use its power and influence to persuade the major Asian states to avoid their own nuclear arms race.

THE WORLD'S POLICEMAN

The present generation is not responsible for the widespread loss of innocent life in Vietnam. Indeed the revulsion has been so complete that that kind of war is unlikely to be repeated in any form. The far harder problem is the temptation to respond to impassioned appeals for intervention to prevent "crimes against humanity" in various places around the world. It is not easy to turn a blind eye to the streams of refugees seen on television or a deaf ear to the stories of murder, arson, and rape, especially when Christian churches are at risk. But ex-colonial countries remember that it was just such events that landed European countries with new colonies. They went in to stop tribal violence and end the slave trade, and then had to police the territory and pour in money, and the best talent of the country went overseas to administer justice.

It was a thankless task and, in my youth, I argued that the under-performance of Britain's economy was due to this diversion of our efforts to our colonies.

Happily, Europe respected the Monroe Doctrine and left the Caribbean and South America to the United States. Once the border between Mexico and Texas was settled, and after the Spanish-American War, there was no more trouble until the Cuban missile crisis, which affected us all. The Europeans do make occasional inquiries. They have questioned U.S. policy in places such as Nicaragua and Grenada. But Europeans accepted that the Monroe Doctrine made Central and South America the backyard of the United States, and that we had problems enough of our own.

The Europeans' own backyard has been and still is the Balkans, the region that was recovered from the Turkish Empire at the end of the nineteenth century by nationalist uprisings. Otto von Bismarck, Germany's first chancellor, said, "The Balkans are not worth the blood of a single Pomeranian grenadier." He hosted the Congress of Berlin, which settled the boundaries of that region, but his successors ignored his advice to keep out and plunged Europe into World War I.

In this sinful world, people will fight each other, and it is not possible for major powers to keep the peace everywhere. It is certainly not possible to keep the peace by inaccurate bombing from twenty thousand feet. Ground cannot be recovered without ground troops, and ground troops mean deaths and body bags. If we threaten but will not risk casualties, then our credibility is reduced to zero. And some civil wars do not end mutual hatred but only make it worse.

With the end of the Cold War, the West has to decide how far it is prepared to go to keep the peace. The breakup of Yugoslavia was a critical event between the old Cold War and the new democratic central Europe. All the other central European countries had thrown off their communist regimes, only Yugoslavia remained. The citizens of the two western Yugoslav provinces, Slovenia and Croatia, made their bid for freedom by declaring independence from Yugoslavia, and there was pressure in Europe to recognize them without asking too closely whether they were viable independent states or, the most critical unasked question, what would happen when Bosnia, which was ethnically divided three ways, also declared independence. Europe once more forgot Bismarck and, with U.S. and Canadian help, began to police the violence in Bosnia and later in Kosovo.

Formally, all European troops are under NATO command; but, after Bosnia, the United States began to feel that it would be better for the European Union to look after its own backyard. So the Europeans proposed their own "rapid reaction force." Then there seemed to be second thoughts in Washington about a force that was not under the immediate direction of the NATO commander in chief, who is always an American.

The difficulty about disengagement from the role of world policeman is that there are vested interests that want to keep the role. And there are security agencies that feed on fear. Back from visits to a bankrupt Russia, which could pay neither its defense industry employees nor its armed forces, our aged host at a lunch in the U.S. Senate said that he had heard from security sources, "which I ought not to disclose," that the Russians were beginning to rearm. It is odd that, by contrast, no security sources in the West forecast the collapse of the Soviet regime ahead of 1989–1990.

NATO was set up half a century ago in another world. The countries of Western Europe were faced by a hostile Soviet Union, which tried to blockade Berlin and had sent in its tanks to put down a democratically elected Czech government. The declared aim of the Soviets was to spread communist power to the rest of Europe. It was the determination of the West, and of America's leadership in particular, that stopped Soviet aggression in its tracks. But once one superpower has gone, there is no longer any need for the remaining superpower to police the rest of the world. The swift and effective response to September 11 does not breach that principle.

"Give to Caesar What Is Caesar's, and to God What Is God's"

None of us like paying taxes any more than the Jews did in the time of Jesus, especially since their taxes went to their Roman overlords, and the local tax-collectors were allowed to take a large slice on the way. But when Christ was asked whether it was right to pay taxes to Caesar or not, he asked, in return, whose head was on the coin. They said, "Caesar's." So Christ said that they should give to Caesar what was Caesar's.

Until the 1980s, the governments of Britain and the United States had tried to balance two separate priorities: the need to maintain the value of their currencies and the need to maintain a high rate of employment. From the 1980s on, they dropped the priority given to employment, which was said to be a matter for business and not for government. But in our highly organized economies, the majority of us have to earn a living by working for a business, and the ability of business to employ us depends on the growth of the economy. Government alone is strong enough to affect the rate of economic growth and the level of employment.

In the last two decades of the twentieth century, British and American governments were determined not to raise taxation as a regulator of economic growth, so they had to rely on their ability to adjust interest rates. In a greedier society, the government's lowering of taxation was hugely popular. Though employment was high and the rich grew richer, the gap between the rich and poor, especially in the cities, was stark. Most of our prosperity comes from our own hard work, but when the froth of our spending comes from borrowing, we put ourselves into the hands of our creditors, and our independence of action is lost. We will find eventually that it does not pay to be too greedy.

The biggest argument against using taxation as a regulator is that most services we need should be provided by a competitive market and not by expensive bureaucrats. But, like it or not, business needs some regulation. Someone has to make sure that our food is safe to eat and that automobiles are safe to drive and travel at a safe speed; that planes are safe to fly, airports have safe landing systems, airways safe guidance systems; that power systems will not black out cities and towns, that public contracts are competitive and free of graft, that there are national highway systems to carry the traffic, and that the accounts of major corporations are honest.

The Western democracies also try to ensure, some more successfully than others, that they have a public health system that will give the same service as private health care, and a public education system that will give the same education and opportunities to the poor as to the rich. The toleration of taxes high enough to pay for it all varies from country to country, as does the gap between rich and poor. We Christians should support policies that narrow that gap.

Protecting the Citizen

Since the days when President Teddy Roosevelt curbed the monopolies of the "robber barons," governments have tried to see that too much industrial power is not concentrated in too few hands and that there is real and fair competition in the marketplace. The federal government case against Microsoft showed that, though not used as much recently, that power is still there.

We will look, in later chapters, at the work of government in negotiating foreign trade deals and in helping to set up regulatory bodies to see that trade is fair as well as free. We will also look at the case for joint action with other governments to protect the environment. Christians especially should encourage efforts to limit damage to the balance of nature. We believe that God has given us the earth in trust, and that each generation must leave it a better place for the next. With a rapidly rising world population, this is probably one of the biggest problems we face, and it is not an easy one on which to get agreement.

FOREIGN POLICY

Last but not least, governments are responsible for foreign policy. This may not rate very high with most citizens. We are all aware of the quarrels within our own country; but other countries, especially those that speak another language, seem to be "over the horizon." If that is true for most countries, it is especially true for America, separated from most of the world by two mighty oceans. But like it or not, America is a superpower, and how America acts matters to people all around the world.

The reconstruction of postwar Europe and the establishment of democracies in place of dictatorships was the result of the American and Canadian generosity that funded the Marshall Plan. By contrast, the mean attitude of the "Group of Seven" (the "G-7") rich countries in refusing more than minimal help to Russia and Ukraine after the collapse of the Soviet Union produced a dangerously unstable Eastern Europe. A more generous America could have led its partners the other way.

Power has its place. Britain had just enough fighter aircraft on September 15, 1940, when Fighter Command threw in its last reserves and prevented the Nazi invasion. American power held the Soviets at the Iron Curtain until communism collapsed. But great power and great wealth can cause resentment among those who have neither.

This is especially true in the arena of Christian missions. A good church needs neither political power nor wealth; and it is best if, when there are enough good churches, they grow on their own, without the visible support of Western churches. Only after Western missionaries had to leave China in the 1940s did the Chinese church begin to grow to its present size. And churches in poorer countries have a lot to teach us. It was the African bishops who kept the last Lambeth Conference of Episcopal churches to its traditional doctrines on sexual relations.

The religious lines today are not so clearly drawn as they were during the Cold War, when the communist states were explicitly anti-Christian. In the Gulf War, the West was defending states where Christians are severely restricted, from attack by Iraq, a state that has freedom of religion and a sizeable Christian church, as have Lebanon, Jordan, and Egypt. Turkey, too, though predominantly Islamic, is a secular state with a growing Christian church.

But official policies of toleration are not always enough to protect the church. In some countries in Africa, Christians are under pressure from Islam; and in India they have been attacked by militant Hindus. Yet it does Christians no good in their own country if they are thought to be allied to and dependent on a foreign power. I have found it more helpful to make the case for religious liberty in meetings like the Euro-Arab dialogue, where individual politicians meet face-to-face; or to talk, on a personal basis, to a minister or local governor, most of whom are strongly opposed to their own militant fundamentalists.

THE PRESENT PUBLIC HOSTILITY TO THE CHRISTIAN CHURCH

But it is not just in the non-Western world that Western Christianity is resented. We should ask ourselves how a country such as the United States, whose institutions and ideals have been so influenced by the Christian faith, has come to treat

Christianity as no more than some sort of doubtful sect, and how the new faith in secular humanism has come to dominate the public institutions that formerly protected a moral and social order grounded in Christianity. A "secular state" is not a state without religion. It is a state that does not give official recognition to any one church. America's founding fathers did not repudiate the Christian faith. They wanted, rightly, a separation of church and state, in contrast to the European countries in the eighteenth century, each of which had their own state church. Even had America's founders been so inclined, it would have been impossible for them to have one state church on the old European system. But the underlying ethos of the Declaration of Independence, though secular in form, is Christian in content. And on the big issues it has stood the test. Slave owners may not have believed that "all men are created equal," but because the vast majority of Americans held the Christian view that people all were indeed equal in God's sight, that view was finally accepted in every state.

America's greatness sprang from its Bible-reading founders. All their motivation is right there in the Bible: the work ethic; the restraint in spending, which created savings; the trust, which encouraged investment and trade; the scientific method of testing all theories by practical experiments in "the book of God's works." In the Bible, America's fathers found the belief that everyone had talents to be developed. They set up schools and universities to give everyone their chance. Out of that came America's fabled technology and management skills and also the respect for the individual, which opened up any job to those who had the talent. And would the slaves have been set free if there had not been such a strong Christian conscience? Would there be equality between all ethnic groups but for the teaching of the Christian faith that God's people are from every tribe, language, people, and nation?

So what has gone wrong? Why has the American constitution not been able to preserve the faith that inspired it? Why has the secular form of the American constitution, its deliberate avoidance of a state church, its anxiety to accommodate the different Christian traditions, been perverted into an instrument actually used against the Christian faith itself?

What has happened is that the new beliefs of secular humanism have asserted themselves as an alternative religion—an alternative to Judaism and Islam as well as to Christianity. Secular humanists are an intellectual elite whose perverted idea of freedom is to allow the merchants of pornography and violence to launch a flood of magazines, books, videos, films, and television programs that debase both men and women and that destroy the institution which, above all others, holds society together in mutual obligation—the family. And having lifted censorship on all that poison, they have latterly had the audacity to want to censor the public appearance of any symbols of the age-old Christian festival on December 25.

The founding fathers decided that the new United States should not have a state church as the English did. Elsewhere in the West, the special position of the remaining state churches has faded. But if the state is not to recognize any one church or even any one religion, it should not adopt any special moral code such as that of secular humanism; and it certainly should not support the objections of secular humanism to the public teaching or recognition of the faith of the majority of its founding fathers. The church can make its own case in the open market of ideas and does not need to ask the state for restrictions similar to those demanded by the secular humanists.

The practical test for the United States—and for any government—is what belief can help provide a healthy moral order to underpin the nation's social order. Secular humanism is not organized strongly enough to encourage fellow citizens to behave well toward each other. It has no networks to help single mothers or fatherless children. Its permissive philosophy has encouraged the breakup of the family, which has been the cause, not the cure, of social instability. Secular humanism depends on the state to enforce its codes of political correctness by new laws, and the state has to bear the extra burden of their enforcement!

By contrast, with pulpits and Sunday schools in every town and city district, the Christian church should certainly qualify as the preserver of the nation's moral health. And the more the church is looking after the homeless, the fatherless, and the prisoners, as Christ taught, the more the state should encourage its efforts.

4

DEMOCRACY

"So God created man in his own image . . . male and female he created them."
GENESIS 1:27

"We here highly resolve . . . that government of the people, by the people, for the people, shall not perish from the earth."
PRESIDENT ABRAHAM LINCOLN
AT GETTYSBURG, 1883

THE DEMAND FOR DEMOCRACY

In the weeks after the presidential election of 2000, America was divided. On the one side were legal deadlines, on the other the democratic issue of whether all the votes should be counted. The legal deadlines won by a narrow margin, because the rule of law must prevail. But there will be a lot more insistence in the future on counting all the votes, because the heart of democracy is the belief that every citizen counts.

We mock elected politicians too easily as the inhabitants of that self-centered world "inside the Beltway"; but we are the people who put them there. What gets us mad is that politics seems to be all talk and little action. If we are Christians, we take the moral high ground against all the laws which, we believe, undermine the moral fiber of our country. Some of us lose patience and take to the streets in protest. But democracy takes into account all points of view and then tries to find a trade-off among them, so it is the essence of democracy that no one group can ever be completely satisfied.

This democratic duty to take account of all views is very different from the duty of the church, which deals in absolute issues of right and wrong. The political process has to judge whether enough people will back a new law to make sure that it is enforced. But the trade-off between what is right and what is enforceable has to stop somewhere. Prohibition of the sale of alcohol was found to be unenforceable, but few people dare face the consequences of the free sale of heroin. There is a point at which a moral judgment asserts itself, however hard it is to enforce the law.

Christians have for the moment lost the public argument against abortion on demand. But we are more likely to regain the ground we have lost if we are seen to be doing all we can to help those pregnant women who want advice, or who want, in the face of family opposition, to keep their child. For then we are talking about reality, not just about ideas. And those who look after people dying of AIDS, abandoned by their "friends" and family, have some authority when they comment on different lifestyles. We will win the public debate by caring for our neighbors in need, not by shouting louder.

A free society is one in which we argue out all these issues privately with our friends and, if we feel strongly enough, write to the local newspaper or to our member of Congress, and what we think and say is reflected by the pollsters and in the press and on television. Then some case hits the headlines and brings the issue into focus and the administration sends a bill to Congress. There the debate is sharpened, the issues are clarified, and minds are gradually addressed to the need for action.

The democratic process is slow because of the need to take everyone's views into account, not just the views of the lobbyists driving a particular issue. And if we are impatient, we need to think of the alternative: a society in which the press is obedient to the government, where debate and discussion are suppressed, where decisions are autocratic and arbitrary, and where the bottom line is the government's determination to keep its grip on political power.

The alternative to democracy is grim. In Europe we lived for a long time right alongside countries with autocratic government, and we knew the difference. I once went with a military driver straight through Checkpoint Charlie in the Berlin Wall. On the western side were the shops, cafes, newsstands, and bustling traffic and crowded pavements of the Kurfurstendamm. Just a minute or so later we were in an eerie silence on the eastern side—no shops, no cafes, no newsstands, no traffic, and hardly any people in the middle of the capital city of East Germany. A new generation must not forget what autocracy was like.

Although the history of democracy in central Europe had been patchy, there was no doubt what the Poles, Czechs, Hungarians, and East Germans wanted. They tuned in to West European radio, and most managed to pick up television too. Just a hundred or so miles away was the free society for which they longed.

In 1956 the Hungarians were the first to rise, but the Russians sent in the tanks and executed their new prime minister. A generation later, as the Iron Curtain began to shake, the Hungarians were the first to test it. They let a trickle of East Germans through to Austria, and soon the trickle became a flood. But by 1989 the Soviet Union no longer had the strength to send in tanks, and soon the Berlin Wall was smashed and new governments committed to democracy took over in East Germany, Hungary, Czechoslovakia, and Poland.

Before that, the European Union's southern neighbors—Portugal, Spain, and Greece—had all exchanged autocratic regimes for democracies. There too, people wanted both the freedom that they saw in the neighboring European Union and also the economic success that seemed to be part of the free society. All three countries have done well since they changed course and joined the European Union.

The Benefits of Freedom

There is clearly a direct connection between democracy and economic success. One reason is that free and open democratic societies give governments feedback on the results of their policies. It used to be part of my political life to meet delegations from around the world. The minister of trade in one large and autocratic country told us that "all the people of our country are behind the government's new trade policy." I wondered how she could possibly know. Her officials would tell her, of course, but how could they tell her anything else? Even if they honestly thought the whole people were behind the policy, how could they be sure? If I were a citizen in such a country, and were asked by an official whether I supported the government's policy, I should nod vigorously—what else? Autocratic governments fill the gap with security police, but the security police become a power to themselves and have their own agenda. So autocratic rulers cannot rely on what *they* say either.

Even if autocratic rulers had an accurate broad-brush feedback on their policies, it would not be enough. Industrial society is extremely complex and also fast-changing. I sat with the communist East German trade minister at the Leipzig Fair, trying to persuade him to allow our exporters to talk directly to the users of the plant we were selling them instead of to the officials of his ministry. Unlike his officials, I explained, the plant managers could understand the technical improvements, which would make all the difference to the cost and quality of their products. He smiled and said, "I do not think that you or I, sitting in this room, are going to be able to change the system." Small wonder that East German industry collapsed when East and West Germany were united ten years later. Democratic freedom of speech, which we take for granted, allows producers to promote their goods in a free market and then let the buyer decide.

For the Christian church, *religious* freedom is even more important. Christians welcome the free market of ideas because, over two thousand years, their faith has won the battle for hearts and minds. It is only when the Christian church has been joined together with political power or has tried to exercise political power itself that, in the spirit of antichrist, it has persecuted those who are not Christians. Christians have survived persecution in China, where Christianity is now reported to be 50 to 90 million strong. Fascism and communism have both disappeared from Europe, but the Christian church has survived there, and the free market in ideas has now returned.

THE CHRISTIAN ORIGINS OF DEMOCRACY

Democracy, like natural science, started in countries where people began to read the Bible for themselves. The death of God the Son for all who trusted him gave all men and women, whatever their race, a new dignity. If God Almighty cared for a beggar, a cripple, a woman of the streets, then every single person was important. And if they were so important to God that his Son died for them, then they are important as citizens of their country too.

Democracy is as much a part of the Protestant ethic as the hard work, saving, and scientific method, and it also made its first appearance in the seventeenth century. In the Reformation, the Lutherans were protected by the Protestant princes; and, except for the short reign of Queen Mary, the Anglicans were protected by the Tudor monarchs. But the Calvinists in Switzerland, France, Scotland, and the Netherlands had a democratic form of church government, based on their view of the "priesthood of all believers" (see 1 Pet. 2:9). And as we have seen, it was a short step from the right to appoint their own elders to the belief that they should also appoint their own rulers. It was the brusque reply of King James I, "No bishop, no king," that sent the Pilgrim fathers off to set up their own community on the bleak coast of America.

These Protestants had all read the Bible for themselves, and it spoke of men and women made in the image of God and directly accountable to God for all they did and said. This feeling of the dignity and personal accountability of everyone, they believed, was plainly contrary to the upper-class insistence that the rest of the people should all do as they were told.

They had all, of course, also read Paul and Peter's rule that Christians should obey "the powers that be." In England, the Parliament resisted the new claims of the king, who took up arms against them. In the short run the civil war settled nothing, and in 1660 the monarchy was restored. But in 1688 the king's successor was displaced when the Parliament sent for a Dutch king and the "English revolution" established the supremacy of Parliament, though a parliament elected by universal suffrage had to wait.

Within a hundred years came the American Declaration of Independence and the first and greatest democracy. Fast-forward to the end of the nineteenth century and all the Protestant nations were democracies.

Our secular society tends to date democracy from the "Enlightenment" and the French Revolution. But that revolution was inspired as much by the French troops returning home from the American War of Independence and by the tyranny of the Bourbon kings as by any intellectual ideas. And the idealism soon vanished in the worse tyranny of the revolutionaries and the dictatorship of Napoleon. Before long the Bourbons were back, and the French coined the saying, "Plus ça change, plus c'est la même chose" ("The more it changes, the more it is the same thing").

"The Price of Liberty Is Eternal Vigilance"

Not even the United States, the world's first democracy, should take democracy for granted. Democracy is vulnerable to forces such as racism, widespread unemployment, breakdown of law and order, and the corruption of the democratic process. Put any two of these together and there could be real danger. So it is well to go back to the underlying ideals and beliefs of the people who brought democracy into being and to recognize, even if it is against the spirit of our age, that those ideals and beliefs spring directly out of the Christian faith.

Democracy has a lot going for it. People want a say in their government. It is a lot easier to govern with the consent of the people than without it. As we have seen, such a consensual arrangement enables feedback, telling government which policies are working and which are not. It avoids the disruption of coups d'etat and revolutions and, combined with the rule of law, gives certainty for business investment and the prosperity which that brings. We ought never to take our freedom for granted, and those we elect ought never to take the voters for granted. Temporary majorities ought not to press strictly partisan policies, since it undermines support for democracy.

All through history, money and power have had no trouble at all in getting along with one another. People use money to get power and they also use power to get money. Read the dire threats of the Old Testament prophets against those in power who use it to add "house to house and . . . field to field" (Isa. 5:8). The only difference today is that both money and power are a lot more ambitious.

The arrival of television gave politicians a far more direct contact with the voter than they ever had through radio or press, so time on television became critical to winning elections. But its cost was way above any cost candidates used to pay. In Europe, candidates have strict limits on campaign costs, and television appearances are free—rationed, but free. But in America it all has to be paid for, and there seems to be no limit to the amount that politicians and their wealthy supporters are willing to pay.

The cost of the presidential campaign in 2000 beat all records. Worst of all, those rich donors who bankrolled the primaries decided which candidates went forward to the party conventions. The grassroots supporters were reduced to rubber stamps. The buying of power by the rich is corruption in any language.

If big donors can short-circuit the vital process of selecting the most powerful officer in the country, leaving all the elected party officers out in the cold, it cannot be long before the ordinary person loses trust in the democratic process. The huge advantage of democracy over other systems is that it legitimizes power. Government can say, "You put us here to do a job and you have to support us in doing it." So, in tough times, governments can take the hard decisions needed and democracies can pull through. But if people believe that the rich have bought the presidency, the Senate, or the House, then democracy is fatally damaged.

The electoral system must enable us to elect political leaders who will not use their position to browbeat the press and television, intimidate the citizen, bribe their way back to power, miscount votes, or call in the army if, despite all that, the vote goes against them. All of this happens in so-called democracies around the world.

What is so dangerous in Western democracies in the early

twenty-first century is the abandonment of the original Christian foundation. A Christian-based democracy should put a high value on truth. God keeps his promises and insists that we keep ours. Are we amused, outraged, or maybe just resigned when political leaders tell us lies? We seem to have redefined truth. We have certainly redefined freedom. It is no longer freedom within a strong self-discipline, based on a strong faith; it is freedom from the key commitments that bind society together, the commitment to truth and the commitment of husband and wife to each other and to their children. But if we insist on the freedom to break those basic commitments, then why should politicians not tell lies to get elected? We depend on the promise of our employer to pay our wages, on customers to pay their debts, on those who guarantee the safety of our aircraft, roads, bridges, and food. We depend on the professional integrity of the doctor and surgeon, on the integrity of our press and our television—at least up to a point! And, however much we criticize them, we want to call to account any politician who tells us lies. We certainly do not want them to be bought by big business, to make decisions that they know to be against the interest of those who elected them.

Rule of the Majority, Consent of the Minority

Democracy, it has been said, is the rule of the majority with the consent of the minority. One warning signal of waning minority consent is a lower voter turnout, which shows that increasing numbers no longer trust in the political process. A further warning comes when the discontented take to the streets because the political system does not seem to hear them. The last stage is when peaceful protest turns to violence.

I will never forget arguing with a packed hall of Protestant students in Queens University, Belfast, that they had a reforming prime minister and that if they abandoned the debate inside the

Unionist Party to take to the streets instead, they would soon find their marches taken over by hard men who understood the streets better than they did. They said that there was no point in arguing with the bigots in the party, who would only take notice when the television showed their street demonstrations. They soon found out that there were no shortcuts, and it took thirty years of violence before the province saw peace again. Northern Ireland's troubles show that democracy does not work unless the rule of the majority has the steady consent of the minority.

The big danger in our materialistic society is that, while the rich majority get richer, the poor get more desperate. There are today people who only just survive on low wages, and others whose whole lives have been disrupted because cheap imports put their industry out of business. The plight of the inner cities is made worse by the breakup of the family, producing poor kids whom no one wants and no one loves. The streets of the big cities are no longer safe, and many new estates are guarded by steel fences and locked gates. Outside the gates are the dispossessed. They have nothing to live for but the next fix, and no way of funding it except to rob.

Someday, the way we are going, someone will organize the dispossessed as Hitler organized the small men who had lost their jobs in Germany between the wars. He will make them feel important and give them something to live for—and even to die for. What would make that citizens' army easier to mobilize in America than in Europe is the right of every American to bear arms. Guns had to be smuggled into Ireland. In America they are in plentiful supply.

The Christian way is not only safer, it is right. It is not only dangerous, but also wrong, to remove hope from any large section of society. Christ cared especially for the sick, the poor, and the social outcast. Any Christian church should have the same priorities, and Christian citizens should do their best to insist that Congress and the presidency have those priorities as well.

The gulf between those who can afford health care and those who have to wait their turn from the overcrowded resources of the free health sector is as wide as ever. None of us who profess our loyalty to the great healer of the lame, the blind, the paralytic, and the lepers should be content with this awful gulf in our rich society.

KEEPING MINORITIES IN THE POLITICAL SYSTEM

The best way of keeping racial or religious or political minority groups from resorting to violence is to bring them into the political system. The political constitution of the United States was based on the needs of its citizens in the late eighteenth century. Then, it was a nation of thirteen states with a population not much bigger than that of Ireland. Today there are fifty states and a population of 270 million. Then, the voters were from a common European background, mainly English, Scots, Dutch, and French Huguenot, all overwhelmingly Protestant. Each state was a minority in the federation, and the main political problem was the balance between the federation and the states. In the first century of the Union, the greatest constitutional problem was the minority who were still slaves. It took a civil war to settle the problem in law and another hundred years to settle it in practice. The problem of the Native American minority was settled more brutally.

The problem of an impoverished minority did not hit the Union for a long time because of the vast natural resources and because, as the country was populated coast to coast, the Protestant ethic developed new industry and commerce. Only at the beginning of the twentieth century, when the owners of industry began to exploit their monopolies, was there any reaction from the workers. But the problem was met by the antitrust laws. The constitution stayed the same.

At the time of the bicentennial of the American constitution, it was my job to write one of the reports for the European Parliament as we aimed to turn the European Community into the European Union. It seemed to me that the U.S. constitution was still one of the best constitutions in the democratic world. The separation of powers is much stronger there than it is elsewhere. No administration can bully or bribe the Congress. The separation between the Union and the States is a model for all democracies. Candidates for Congress have to reside in their district; that, and biennial elections, keep them in close contact with their constituents.

But the U.S. electoral system squeezes out the smaller parties who would otherwise represent minorities. Britain's old constitution, its shape set in 1832, is the only other that keeps to that same system. All the newer systems that I studied make sure that the balance of the legislative body roughly reflects the balance of the overall national vote. So the most important minority parties are included, and it is rare for any one party to have an overall majority; usually, a major party wins by forming a coalition with at least one smaller party.

Ireland uses a voting system of multi-member districts, which allocates seats in rough proportion to the votes cast. So, instead of just two parties being represented, minority parties get members too. Northern Ireland has this system for the European Parliament elections and, without it, the Nationalists would not have been represented. Britain now uses a similar system for the European Parliament, and all European countries use a system that gives minority parties seats in both national and European parliaments. The older democracies of the United Kingdom and the United States are exceptions in sticking to systems that exclude minority parties. The primaries give a wider choice, but only within the party framework.

The two-party system forces each party to try to hold together people of quite different views; but the bargains are behind closed doors and leave an image of politicians promising one thing and doing another. The United States has very low voter turnout, a sure sign of citizens who feel left out of the democratic process.

And maybe it is not only the poor, but Christians too, who feel left out.

How Can Christians Make a Difference?

There are Christians who want to take over the party to which they belong. A church in England had the bright idea of signing up its members for the Conservative Party just ahead of the meeting that appoints the officers, and they found themselves in charge right after the meeting. But it is doubtful whether the church will be able to turn out the vote, especially since a well-known journalist has promised to represent the old Conservatives.

In America it is possible for minorities, including those holding strong Christian views, to wage primary election campaigns for a candidate who represents their point of view. But it is hard for a newcomer to stand against the sitting member, who has more experience, constant access to local press, radio, and television, and far more credibility when asking for election funds. I had a long talk with Senator Mark Hatfield before he retired. We agreed that the only effective way of getting a Christian view into legislation was to win the argument in the country. Christian legislators can and should vote with their consciences. And we can explain our views in public. But we cannot expect our colleagues to fly in the face of established public opinion. It is the duty of Christians in the electoral districts to change the views of their neighbors. It can be done, but it has to be done in a Christian way.

The early Christians did not convert the Roman Empire by lobbying pagan emperors; they did it by being such good neighbors that those living around them were impressed by their neighborly love (Christ's second commandment). Within three hundred years they had overcome pagan religion and Greek philosophy, and the Emperor had declared himself a Christian. Within another hundred years, the pagan tribes came across the Alps and destroyed the Empire, but the Christians did not give up; they planted missions and looked after the sick, the children, the old, and the travelers, and won the hearts and minds of the Goths, Franks, Scots, Angles, Saxons, Danes, and Slavs, who left their pagan gods and were baptized as Christians. Our backward looks seldom go beyond the corruption of the medieval church to the enormous gains of those simple, loving churches of the first millennium.

We have such churches today. I opened the extension of a church in a rough part of Liverpool. It had a great outreach to those in need all around it, arousing the attention of the mayor, who came looking tired as she arrived for another engagement on a busy program. But she was so impressed as she listened that she canceled her next engagement to stay on to see more of the church's social work. Later she asked some of those who took part to visit her in the city hall. I wrote an account on a similar outreach by another church in a small industrial town and sent it to the Socialist Member of Parliament, a tough character if ever there was one. She went to see it and was greatly impressed. We had a meeting of the churches in Derby, where Rolls Royce airplane engines are made, to see if we could get church support in networking their social action. The mayor welcomed us and told us that the city authorities badly needed the help of churches in dealing with all the social problems of the city.

Today's secular social theory, which influences our politicians within the Beltway, is cut off from the realities of life. But back in their electoral districts, congressmen are face-to-face with social breakdown and all the trouble it brings. And when they see the churches dealing with problems that are beyond the capacity of the city halls, they will listen less to the social think tanks and more to those whose love and care is solving the problems that social theory has created. And the more Christian politicians can report about what the church is doing, the more their colleagues will listen to what we are saying.

DEMOCRACY KEEPS GOVERNMENT CLOSE TO THE PEOPLE

For fifteen years I was the member of the European Parliament for the English county of Cambridgeshire, which is about the same size as a U.S. congressional district. Like an American congressman, I lived in the district I represented, and it was a great feeling to be responsible for your own friends and neighbors. I answered every letter and dealt with every problem, however tough or complicated. I tried to spend several days a month traveling through the district, speaking in schools, going to party functions, walking around industrial plants, and always visiting the local newspaper and radio station. Democracy is the human connection between the citizen and the huge, distant, and impersonal business of government.

All doors are open to the elected member, all advice available. Cambridge University had the country's leading expert on the safety of nuclear power, another senior faculty member was a very helpful expert on genetic engineering, and the university had some brilliant economists. Help was there whenever it was needed.

The university's open and active support of the development of high-tech products had spawned a rapid growth of high-tech industry around the city. I tried to understand as much as I could; but though I grasped the need for "tools" for testing software, I could not begin to understand how they did their job! As I listened to the export problems of these very successful high-tech companies, I realized that though this was supposed to be a "common market," it was not. Tariffs were not the only possible barrier to trade. I heard the same story at a lunch with the American Chamber of Commerce in Brussels, which represented larger corporations.

So I got together with the four other presidents of the economic committees of the Parliament, of which I was one, and we persuaded the president, Piet Dankert, to let us commission a report on the best way forward. A grand committee considered the report and held major "hearings," the Parliament voted for its recommendation that we abolish all remaining barriers to a truly single market, the member states agreed, and the administration was told to get on with it. That is the kind of feedback given by a democratic system.

Talking around these small high-tech companies, I also realized that though the big companies could cope with exchange risk, the small ones could not. Looking at the effects of the single market, it was also clear that in a completely open market in goods and services, where some countries would run surpluses and others deficits, the present system was not strong enough to stand up to the currency speculators; we needed a single currency and, with the flourishing export trade of the high-tech companies in Cambridgeshire, I supported this.

The member states did not handle this as well as they handled the idea of a single market. They saw it as a technical problem to be solved behind closed doors by central bank governors, and they did not go through the parliamentary channels to get political support. The Danes and British, both with strong democratic traditions, opted out; and before the new system was firmly in place, there was a run on the currencies of the countries in trade deficit, as the Parliament had predicted. But today, the new single currency, the euro, is near parity with the dollar.

THE RULE OF LAW

Every few years, democracy demands that our powerful rulers step down and make way for their opponents. That can only happen in a country where law reigns supreme; in most countries in the world, governments will not give up power. The rewards of power and the riches it brings are too great and the fear of reprisals too fearsome—and if the rule of law has to be broken in order to maintain one's power, then so be it.

We do not have to look farther than the Old Testament prophets to find the rule of law being flouted by the rich and powerful. Israel had a strict law of family inheritance, aimed at making sure that all citizens had their own land. King Ahab wanted his neighbor Naboth's vineyard, and when Naboth refused, Ahab's wife Jezebel had him killed. The prophet Elijah told Ahab that the dogs would lick his blood on the ground where Naboth died (1 Kings 21).

The rule of law not only protects the poor from the rich and powerful but also gives the assurance that suppliers get paid for what they deliver, and that what customers receive from suppliers is what was ordered and that it will do the job. Without that assurance, the whole rich stream of production and trade—and our high incomes—would wither away.

The prosperity of the West has lasted so long that it seems ridiculous to talk of failure. But we have to watch out. In a large part of the world, might is right; and if our rule of law fails, then we will go the same way. The danger is real. The tide of opinion is set strongly against the supporting principle of right and wrong on which our laws are based. Our permissive society has no absolutes; everything is relative. But a bill for $21,240 demands a check for $21,240—no less. There is nothing relative about our salary check at the end of the month. And if promises don't count in the bedroom, why should they count in the boardroom? Why should we rely on any assurances?

We are promised that our food is safe to eat and our automobile safe to drive. There is nothing relative about automobile accidents or food poisoning. Investors want to know whether a corporation's accounts are a fair view of its financial position. The rising tide of litigation shows that we are no longer so sure about all these promises. But litigation is no substitute for trust. Seniors say to juniors, "Don't worry too much, Son, we can always litigate." Already the proportion of lawyers in the United States is said to be twice as large as in any other country in the West.

Truth breeds trust in the capital markets, and trust breeds business, allowing millions of transactions, worth billions of dollars, every hour. As confidence plunges, so does business. It is a very long way down to the standard of living in countries where there is neither truth nor confidence, but once we are on the way down, it is hard to recover that lost trust.

Democracy Needs a Free, Fearless, and Truthful Press

One great safeguard to truth is a free press. That was why the first contract shooting of a television journalist in Moscow sent shock waves around Russia. Who was now safe from the reach of the new business barons?

The press is not perfect. It can be loud and unfair to the innocent. It can run vendettas and break reputations. It can have owners who have their own agenda and who pursue it tirelessly. Newspapers and television can follow each other's line like a flock of sheep, just because it is easier to go with the tide than against it. Press and television can also be shocking to those who want to maintain some moral standards in society. But, on balance, the press goes after the villains. It is out to uncover hypocrites, to expose shady deals, and to give the lie to political pretensions.

Liars do get found out. Sleazy politicians do get exposed. Windy rhetoric is punctured or ignored. I do not know about the American tabloids, but the best of American broadsheets are very good indeed. And on both sides of the pond, we have some very good political television, with sharp interviews and probing questions.

The press responds to the truth. For five years I took the press conference after the monthly meeting of our National Economic Development Council. It was chaired either by the prime minister or the chancellor (our treasury minister), and four other senior ministers sat around the table, with half a dozen each from big business and our largest trade unions. So its meetings were news. I decided early on that, if for safety alone, I would tell it as it was. If one of the three groups objected to the accuracy of what was reported (it happened twice), I could refer them to the other two (and that settled it both times).

Very soon the press conference had a credibility far above that achieved by government, business, or unions, all of whom were suspected of putting on their own spin. This gave the Council's agenda for economic development huge coverage in all of the media. It also led to a good personal relationship with key economic and business journalists and a lot of private exchange of opinion and argument, which went on for several years after I had gone back to industry.

But the press has its weaknesses too. Some press and television barons want to use their position to advance their own political agenda and only hire editors and producers who will give their reporting and opinion that slant. A former British prime minister said of similar press barons, "Like prostitutes down the ages, they have power without responsibility." That was enough to put them in their place. Today's leaders are not so robust, and that allows irresponsible press barons to do much more damage. The solution is either antitrust or new direct laws that limit the coverage of a single owner. Meanwhile those owners who try to push their own views too far are subject to ridicule by brave journalists who are out of their reach.

But even with that caution, the press provides a breath of fresh air to blow away windy rhetoric and to straighten out the spin of government spokesmen. Publicity is a powerful weapon in keeping powerful people in line with the truth. Those with something to hide do not easily get through an open cross-examination. As I am writing, a cabinet minister, who was cross-questioned yesterday on our best television political program, has resigned today. Far more could go wrong were the press not there to expose it. A free press is an essential part of any democratic process.

5

FAIR TRADING

"Honesty is the best policy."
RICHARD WHATLEY,
ARCHBISHOP OF DUBLIN

"You must have accurate and honest weights and measures."
MOSES (DEUT. 25:15)

COMPETITION

At Dulles International Airport, there is a long line of car rental lots, with Hertz, the number one and oldest, at one end, and Alamo, the most recent, at the other end. Competition like this, where we can compare automobiles and prices, gives the best deal for the customer.

Competition made Avis, when number two, sell on the slogan, "We try harder," and it keeps all competitors on their toes. The sharp edge of competition keeps prices down and makes managements look for better products, better customer service, slicker production, and swifter distribution. Competition compels management to recruit and promote on merit and, if they do not, their best staff will find a company that does. Competition on the capital market directs funds to companies with the best financial performance.

But competition has to be fair. The natural instinct of the big guys is to try to lean on the small ones, to keep them in their place or wipe them out altogether. At the end of the nineteenth century, when America was growing fast, that was how the railroad, oil, and steel barons made their money. The trust-busting Sherman Act was passed in the 1890s, but it needed a self-confident president, Teddy Roosevelt, to put it into action. The later Robinson Patman Act forbids corporations to put competitors out of business by discriminatory prices.

But for some time before the Microsoft case, these laws had been little used. Maybe it was because globalization had brought in such strong foreign competition—for instance, Japanese automobiles and electronics—that it was impossible for any one American company to dominate the market. But when Microsoft seemed to dominate even the international market, antitrust swung into action.

Competitive theory is that those who keep their costs lowest can gain business by giving the best deals—either lower prices or better value. But it is not so simple. Business today needs heavy investment in research, development, and new "state of the art" plants. A huge part of the costs has been sunk before the first product comes off the line, and the higher the volume of sales, the faster that sunk cost will be recovered. So there is a temptation in a competitive market to sell at marginal prices, undercut competitors, and get the cash back fast.

Cutting prices to gain volume would bring swift retaliation in the domestic market, but it can be very tempting to get big volume sales by cutting prices in export markets. This process is known as "dumping," and though there are international laws against it, by the time they have swung into action with "countervailing duties," the market has been lost. So, if they can, companies on the losing end gang up and dump right back into the offending market.

Short term, this is expensive, but it soon puts a stop to the dumping. We warned the president of a smaller American producer of aluminum ingot that if they dumped again, we would sell an equivalent amount to his best customer at the same price with 10 percent off. He tried us out and we dumped back. After that, we had no trouble. Then the big Japanese producers dumped, and we dumped right back into the Tokyo market. This brought a shocked delegation from the four Japanese majors, begging us never to do that again and promising that they would never dump again. They kept their word.

There was a time when international trade did not matter to a self-sufficient United States. But that time has long gone, and today it is strongly in America's interests to see that the rules of international trade are fair and that no one exports to America from behind impregnable tariff walls. Successive "rounds" of the General Agreement on Tariffs and Trade (GATT) have lowered tariffs and made the competitive playing field as level as they can manage.

It was not easy to have a level playing field with the communist countries, since they did not have a free internal market and their imports were bought by government departments. There was once an anti-dumping case against a communist country for undercutting the Western market for Christmas cards! Today's Chinese market seems more in the Western mold; but it is still in its early days.

Japan is the one "open" market that has not been fully accessible to foreign companies. The reason is that the great "zaibatsu" trading houses not only control the major corporations but also own the banks and the distribution networks. So while they could cooperate with each other to dominate Western markets for electronics, motorcycles, and automobiles, the West could not get distribution or customer finance to respond with exports to Japan.

Their ability to keep 100 percent of their home market gave Japanese exporters a cash-flow for new investments much greater than that of Western companies, which enabled them to take over major sectors of American and European industry.

America seemed most reluctant to take action. Maybe it was because it felt that Japan was a strategic ally in East Asia—the reaction I got at Foggy Bottom—maybe because it was thought that the Japanese social structure was still too fragile to stand the impact of fierce Western competition. Europe took a more robust line. A senior official of the European Union was sent to Japan to point out that, under the GATT rules, there was a restraint on our exports to Japan. They settled out of court for a quota of 11 percent of the European market in automobiles, which has now lasted for nearly two decades.

Clearly, competition is not perfect. For instance, there are banks whose command of the market seems to allow them to ignore the care of the customer, who can go nowhere else—as described in this story from *The Washington Post:*

> A while back I deposited a substantial check and then paid some bills, figuring the deposited check would clear even before mine were delivered in the mail. But the check I had deposited was OUT OF STATE and only a portion of it would be cleared. A bit later, more of it would be cleared until, many years from now, all the funds would be available.
>
> I tried to call my bank to prevent my checks from bouncing all over town. It turned out, though, that my branch had an unlisted number. I called the bank's main number and ultimately reached a human being. I explained my dilemma. I needed to talk to my branch. What's the number? Sorry, the human being answered, you cannot have the number. But my bank has MY number, I said. It also has my money. I want to talk to the people who have my money.

What's the number? No dice. I could leave my number and someone would get back to me within 48 hours. Two days! By then my checks would be bouncing all over town—and that's what happened.

My bank's slogan is "The right relationship is everything."

And there are computer systems enjoying a quasi-monopoly that are set up by computer buffs who make them do endless clever things while the average customer needs something simpler and more understandable—as described in this letter to a British national paper, the *Independent,* and signed by an Air Force squadron leader:

The more time I spend on my computer, the more I am convinced that they have good days and bad days.

For example, I will shut down the computer at night, having had a good day, expecting the same the following day. But, like a rebellious child it disobeys my instructions and produces inscriptions such as "this program has performed an illegal act," but really meaning you.

You press on, hoping that the mood will change, but often, if you press too hard, the screen will freeze and you are powerless to do anything except simulate a power cut, allowing things to cool down and start up again.

Sometimes this is enough to change the mood, but not always.

Though competition is a good general principle, there are still corners it does not seem to touch. But Christians brought up in the duty of care will always try to put themselves in their customers' shoes.

COOPERATION

To many Christians, competition is a bad word and cooperation a good one. But experience shows that "cooperation" can too easily slip into price-fixing, and our imperfect world needs competition in price, innovation, and quality, to name just a few of the needs of customers. But there is a place for cooperation too.

In each industry there is a huge, lively, and growing body of professional expertise. It draws on and contributes to the body of academic expertise in the universities, including the business schools. Key corporate staff, engineers—nautical, aeronautical, civil, mechanical, and electronic—chemists and physicists, accountants and lawyers, all belong to their professional body. They all owe lifelong allegiance to their profession and to its ethical standards. In an ethical conflict between profession and employer, few would risk their professional reputation. Cooperation in an industry comes through the professional journals, which disseminate the growing body of scientific knowledge. And when they have gained a market advantage, companies are usually happy to share their breakthroughs.

The MBAs from the business schools and the rapidly growing profession of management consultants spread management expertise, and so do the search consultants, who shift the best and brightest to posts where they can do the most good.

More protective of interests and less focused on exchange of expertise, there are the trade associations to keep management in touch across the competitive battlefront. And, above all, there is the steady stream of skilled staff moving from one company to another and taking their expertise with them.

Even the largest European country is only a fraction of the size of the United States and has to make its way in a highly competitive world; but most European countries believe that there is room for even more organized cooperation. The French had their "Commissariat General du Plan," the British their National Economic Development Council (sidelined by a monetarist government in the 1980s and abolished in the early 1990s). The German cities each have their heavily funded chambers of commerce. In Germany, too, the major banks have strong holdings in each of their key companies, and each industry's own trade union is as interested in the success of that industry as a whole as in the success of the individual companies where their members are employed. Japan, too, seems to have owed a great deal of its success to the planning of its Ministry of Trade and Industry (MITI).

This European cooperation between government and industry is part of the Rhine model, in contrast to the arms-length Anglo-Saxon model, which puts much more trust in the market mechanism. In the 1990s the Rhine model was more successful in balancing external trade and less successful than the Anglo-Saxon model in promoting employment. But the high unemployment in the Rhine model countries is heavily concentrated in ex-communist East Germany and in the long-term structural unemployment along the Mediterranean fringe of Spain and Greece.

RELATIONS BETWEEN GOVERNMENT AND INDUSTRY

As a young CEO in the 1960s, I did all I could to encourage a closer relationship between government and industry. I found that civil servants and politicians had no idea of industry's vital microeconomics—what happens inside companies and why. They could, and did, make catastrophic trade concessions without any consultation; they thought that we could change direction as fast as they changed their minds; nor did they understand the ability of workers in highly capitalized industries to hold production lines to ransom.

I was, for seven years, a member of our National Economic Development Council and director general for five. The NEDC had reports from the committees of the Council for each of twenty industries, as well as from economists and civil servants. These down-to-earth industry documents were agreed upon with trade union leaders and had input from the responsible government

departments. So our Council debates were grounded, not on political rhetoric or partisan prejudice, but on the hard facts. The support of the labor leaders, representing millions of voters, gave a
political edge to the advice that corporate management could not
achieve on its own and also gave it a good press, especially in cities
where the industry was concentrated. The Council also recognized that dividends are only a fraction of the payroll and that it
was not only shareholders who had an economic interest in the
future of an industry.

The lively debates were not confined to those around the
Council table. The press conference afterwards had no political
spin, and, as I mentioned in chapter 4, that gave the Council a
media coverage that politicians envied. So, on a far wider front, the
debate moved from windy political rhetoric to practical business
reality. The conditions on which we could keep full employment,
the need to balance our trade, the need for entry into the European
Union, the need for trade union reform and for putting greater
national resources into industrial investment, all became part of
the national debate.

Four years later, Britain, under a new Labour government
which called a referendum, voted two to one to stay in the
European Union and I took over as chairman of our export promotion body, with the job of switching our trade from the old
Commonwealth markets to the new European market. We had
export conferences in eighteen cities. In each city, two local small
businesses and two large, told—with the help of audiovisuals—
their success stories and, chaired by one of our best radio anchor-
men, the conference cross-examined them. Every conference was
packed and made a big local impact. That seemed to me a good
example of cooperation in a competitive world.

Some markets are not as simple as they seem. Whether or not
it was Enron that caused power failures in California, leaving it all

to the market alone has reportedly turned off cooling systems in the hottest weather. It seems fairly clear that the state of California would have benefited from some cooperative planning that brought people together to make sure the power was in place when it was wanted. There are services that need a long planning period to get agreement between the state and all who have to provide the supply, including, if need be, other nearby states. And if Enron was the problem, that would have shown up a lot earlier.

In Britain, the idea of rational discussion with government on the problems and prospects of key industries was at first only opposed from the hard-line right. I had half an hour on national radio with their most articulate spokesman, Enoch Powell—no chair, just the microphone between us. He objected that if businessmen got together with each other, they would rig the market. I answered that if they wanted to do that, they would do it over lunch in the Savoy Grill and not in front of civil servants. Luckily, my watch was more accurate than his, and I had the last word before the green light went off.

But the eighties saw the arrival of a new idea on both sides of the pond: monetarism, whose gurus declared that everything could be solved by the market alone. Interest rates were now the sole regulator—and the base rate went up to 15 percent, and the number of unemployed was higher than in the depression of the thirties. Whole areas of both the United States and Britain became rust belts. The market certainly gave decisive decisions; but it did not answer the two vital problems: how a country could earn a living in a competitive world, and how we could keep our workforce employed.

In the early 1990s, the National Economic Development Council, having been downgraded, was finally abolished. Almost immediately Members of Parliament started to have offers of money in return for their influence, and many did this without declaring the cash. It was one of the factors that helped the Labour Party to get its first election victory in eighteen years.

Politics and the economy are too closely intertwined in modern democracy for governments to ignore the need for reasoned and organized and open dialogue with business; and it is in the interests of business, as well as competing in the market, to cooperate in making government understand the economics of the industries on which the prosperity of their country depends.

TRADE THRIVES ON TRUST

The simple virtue of honesty is at the heart of all successful business. Trade sprang to life in the seventeenth century when people learned to trust the Dutch merchants and Swiss bankers of the new Reformed church. They were still tough businessmen, but when the deal was done, they kept their word. They did not aim to make as much as they could out of each deal. They paid on time and charged low prices and interest rates, so their suppliers, customers, and depositors came back for repeat business. The more business they did, the more they trusted each other. Fast-forward to today: my own experience is that if the Dutch do not think there is enough profit for both parties, they will not do the deal.

Too often in businesses today, with diminishing trust, every major transaction has to have lawyers crawling all over it, and the mood is, "If it goes wrong, we can always litigate." So the threat of litigation begins to slow the pace. Worse, greed encourages deals with known rogues, and the losses, which fall on the still trusting public, do great damage to the credibility of business.

BRIBERY AND CORRUPTION

In most of the world, no one trusts anyone outside their own extended family and the local branches of the Western multina-

tionals. Mutual mistrust is probably the greate
poverty throughout the world.

The corruption that causes this distrust us
hidden. But in 1970s, following the first oil shock, some back
countries found themselves with a huge income and launched
gigantic new projects, each with its demands for bribes on a scale
never before faced by Western business.

I happened to be chair of the British Overseas Trade Board at
the time and was also on the advisory council of the Davos
Management Forum (now the World Economic Forum). So I had
firsthand accounts of the problems, which no one mentioned in
public. Governments professed to know nothing, and business
would say nothing in public; but I thought it unrealistic for someone who was supposed to be heading the country's export drive to
say nothing in public. As we have seen in an earlier chapter, there
were arguments against bribery that had to be made:

- If contracts are awarded on the highest kickback rather
  than the best bid, the process becomes a lottery in which
  competent companies lose out.
- There is endless delay while those due to get the bribe
  argue among themselves as to who gets what. Sometimes
  they cannot agree, and the contract is never awarded.
- Those companies paying bribes are liable to find their own
  staff being offered bribes by local subcontractors, and there
  is then no guarantee that the subcontractor's work is safe
  or that the supplier's product is up to specifications.
- If the bribery is uncovered (as in the Lockheed scandal
  at about that time), the professional careers of all
  involved will be irretrievably destroyed and they will
  never have another position of trust.
- Two-thirds of export markets are free of bribery, and that
  should be enough for any corporation.

- If bribes are needed for permission to build a refinery in a corrupt country, then the investment is a hostage to endless demands throughout its working life.
- Bribery destabilizes governments, since it creates an envious group who also want to make their fortunes and who will, one day, probably stage a successful coup. They will use as an excuse the corruption of the government they have turned out, and, to prove it, will also take action against the companies that have given the bribes. So the payments on a successful contract will only last until the next coup; the company will be on the blacklist forever, and its local staff will be lucky to stay out of jail.

For all these reasons, most of Western industry took a hard line against paying bribes.

The problem of endemic bribery has led most aid organizations to route their funds not to local government but through Western nongovernmental aid organizations ("NGOs"). But even then there can be problems. At a time of famine, one NGO could not get access to the government warehouse where its food aid was stored because the official in charge demanded a bribe. The NGO said it did not have the money, nor was that its practice. Not until the NGO told the president of the country that it would organize an aid embargo was the warehouse opened.

The Old Testament is wholehearted in its condemnations of bribery, which blinds the eyes of the judges and deprives the poor of justice (Ps. 26:10; Prov. 15:27; Isa. 33:15; Amos 5:12). And we should note that the apostle Paul was kept in prison and away from the churches that needed him simply because he would not pay a bribe to the Roman governor Felix (Acts 24:26).

Most businesses will pay the small amounts demanded by poorly paid customs officials for the release of their duty-paid goods from the customs sheds, and will allow their agents to use their judgment on what similar amounts they pay on their own responsibility out of their own commission, so that the "custom of the country"—poorly paid officials—is not entirely ignored.

The heart of corruption is the perversion of justice. If it could get its act together, Western business could do more to prevent it. Corrupt rulers need safe havens for their bank accounts, and it would be a great disincentive to bribery if the Western banking community could take some responsibility for policing the vast funds, from drugs as well as from bribes, that pass through its hands. Offshore accounts in tiny independent principalities are dependent on mainstream banking facilities, and if the banking community and governments were determined, there would surely be some way in which they could act together to fight such corruption.

Since honesty is so vital to the West, governments should also make sure that the incomes of public servants do not fall so far behind the rest of the community that they are tempted to accept bribes. In the early seventeenth century, British judges accepted gifts from litigants as a matter of course. Two centuries later they were paid so well that none of them would risk their post and its income by accepting a bribe. Today it is wise to see that police are paid well enough to put the income stream from the remainder of their service well above any casual bribe.

Those who ask for bribes usually find that corruption devours them. Rulers are deposed by envious men who want their own turn. Even those rulers who escape with their lives have to live in exile far from familiar friends. They may have a wonderful view of the Lake of Geneva, but no one comes to call. The givers of bribes suffer the same social isolation. At a big reception in London, a politician who had once hoped to lead his party stood all alone. He had unwisely accepted a large fee as director of a company that had then been caught giving bribes. He said he knew nothing about it; but why did he not ask those who could have and would have warned him?

BUILDING TRUST

Trust is easily lost. Building trust is a longer job, but one that we all need to take on. If we look at the lives of successful business-men, one of the strongest foundations has always been the repu-tation they gained with their customers. Robert Laidlaw, who built up the largest mail-order business in New Zealand, had to per-suade people to pay good money for goods they had never seen outside the pages of his catalog and to reassure them that there was no need for a sheep farmer to make the long journey into town to see the goods for himself. He also had to persuade them that his catalog would always quote a competitive price, that they would lose no money through ordering by mail, and that the goods they ordered would always arrive on time and would be exactly as described. It was hard work, but even when the pressure was on this new and vulnerable business, he took no shortcuts.

It is sometimes tough to keep delivery dates, to pay on time, to keep within bank credit limits, and to meet hard specifications. It is not always easy to give clients the right advice when they do not want to hear it, to put the downside prospect in a company's annual statement, or to claim no more for the product than it will deliver. But all of this builds trust. Trust leads to repeat orders and repeat financing and builds a long-term business.

There comes a time when people no longer trust the heavy promotion. A long while ago I asked the president of Ford, Arjay Miller, how the small, imported, old-fashioned Volkswagen did so well against the wall-to-wall advertising of the American automo-bile industry. He said simply, "Word of mouth." People trusted their friends rather than the high-powered promotion.

It is important for anyone who wants to build a reputation for trust to start in the right business or profession. When I was young, most Christians kept clear of tobacco, mainly because it was addictive and expensive, but also, in my case, because my sport was rowing and I wanted to keep healthy and strong. But in those days nonsmokers were a small minority who had to put up with dense tobacco smoke in crowded offices. Later in life, I sat at an economic council with the head of our biggest tobacco company among the industrialists, faced, among the trade unions, by a brilliant labor leader who was slowly dying of lung cancer. When I was in my thirties, the most fashionable industry was nuclear power. Now the public trusts neither the tobacco nor the nuclear industry.

Passing fashion is a bad guide to a lifetime career. We should find an industry or profession that is thoroughly useful. Christians especially should want an activity that is socially worthwhile and that sells a product or service because it is really needed. We will not want to sell a product on its appeal to vanity or passing whims, let alone products that are medically and socially harmful.

Trust in Financial Markets

The expert can also exploit the ignorant in financial services, which is why they are surrounded by government regulation as well as stock exchange rules. Human greed makes exploitation easy, not just for the outright fraudster but for those who have put enough in the small print to keep them out of jail.

A friend of ours, a young Scots accountant in the high-tech business, was offered one of the now notorious Enron deals. When he had finally unraveled all the implications of the proposal, he pointed out that the liability of the proposed joint venture would not be shown on Enron's balance sheet. He said that that would not be allowed in Britain, and was assured that it *was* allowed in

America. He and his company were saved by his unshaken belief that, even if American law allowed it, it was morally wrong to hide major liabilities.

Arthur Andersen, Enron's auditors, had already split their consultancy business from their auditing; but the culture of doing what the client wanted had hung on and, as a result, the biggest native American auditing partnership is, at the time of this writing, in meltdown. An auditor's job is to certify that the reported figures of a company are not only "true" but also "fair." If the shareholders, bankers, and creditors of a company cannot rely on that certificate, then the entire process is useless. Our huge capital markets and worldwide trading system must rely on honest reporting or they too will go into meltdown.

I learned my profession from the managers of the great firm of Price Waterhouse, who had been through the financial crash of 1929–1931. Whenever a ruined financier shot himself, they were brought in to find out what had gone wrong. You would have thought markets would have learned the lesson for good. But greedy people are gullible, and it happens again and again. There was the savings and loan scandal. In Britain, there was the property crash of the mid-seventies and the depression of the late eighties. And now one major corporation after another is revising its profits downward and the stock exchange has slumped because investors no longer know whether they can trust any corporation's figures.

Loss of confidence can come very quickly as people begin to panic. The irrationality on the downswing is even worse than it is on the upswing. But always, until now, confidence has returned. There has been enough honesty, enough discipline, enough belief in each other and trust in those who run the system, to swing us back to belief in the system. But we now live in a society that has repudiated the Judeo-Christian moral order—the belief in right and wrong, truth and falsehood—and is off on an arrogant social experiment of its own in which there are no inconvenient absolutes and no one talks about the need for truth and the trust that it brings. That may be convenient if you want to conduct sexual affairs, but it does not hold society together any better than it holds the family together.

LITIGATION IS NO ALTERNATIVE

In the absence of a moral law to protect us, we turn to the civil law and sue each other instead. As truth declines, litigation rises. But no amount of litigation will rescue us from a real crash in confidence. And there is a limit to the volume of litigation that courts can handle.

We need to trust the safety of air travel, surgery, railroads, the police, and the armed services; but nothing can bring such widespread catastrophe in our interdependent society as a loss of confidence in financial markets. The level of the Dow or the purchasing power of the dollar can go down as well as up. If we spend up to the limit of our income, these changes can hurt us. If we lose our income, it is very tough. If millions lose their income all at the same time, it is catastrophic. We depend on the system we have built to provide jobs and to pay for law and order; and if the system crashes, we will all be hurt. Our confidence in the system depends on our confidence that those who run it are telling us the truth.

6

PLAYING THE MARKETS

"The love of money is a root of all kinds of evil."
THE APOSTLE PAUL (1 TIM. 6:10)

"Market fundamentalism has rendered the global capitalist system unsound and unsustainable."
GEORGE SOROS,
THE CRISIS OF GLOBAL CAPITALISM

"Woe to you who add house to house and join field to field till no space is left."
THE PROPHET ISAIAH (ISA. 5:8)

THE USE AND ABUSE OF THE STOCK MARKET

Near the close of the last chapter, I mentioned the bankrupt stockbrokers who committed suicide after the Wall Street crash of 1929. Most of these desperate financiers had cooked the books to pay dividends out of capital. That practice sends the share price soaring and encourages the public to buy new issues. The overpriced shares are also issued to buy new companies for the group, and the addition of their profits creates a soaring group profit, which encourages even more investors to jump on the bandwagon. This process can go on undetected for some time. But with a stock market crash, the game is up. In the 1930s slump, one financier, more careful of his life than others, came to see a partner of Price Waterhouse to ask for his advice. The partner listened and then said, "Here is the telephone, and that is the number of the public prosecutor."

The 1929 crash and the slump that followed gave capitalism a bad name and was one of the causes of Hitler's rise to power in Germany in 1933. In America it led to Roosevelt's "New Deal" and direct government action to increase employment. It also led to new rules on the Stock Exchange to limit trading on margin—that is, borrowing to buy shares against the security of their market value.

But bad habits die hard, and fools are born every day. Thirty years after the Wall Street crash, a new sort of financier arose. It was, by now, far more difficult to pay dividends out of capital. But these financiers convinced the market that they could take over and turn around "sleepy" corporations, despite their knowing nothing about the industry. So there was a sharp rise in hostile bids, financed by "junk bonds," which, though they gave little security, carried a very high interest rate.

One of the most spectacular was the bid by a consortium, led by the late Jimmy Goldsmith, for Goodyear Tire, one of the world's leading tire makers. Goodyear had had a profit setback due to a diversion into the oil pipeline business, of which it had no experience. But that ignorance was marginal compared with the consortium's ignorance of the tire business. Goodyear was forced to defend itself by buying its own shares with very high-interest "junk bonds"—at enormous long-term cost to the business and great gain to the raiders.

This kind of corporate raid, financed by junk bonds, did no good to the reputation of capital markets, and in the end the inventor of junk bonds went too far and found himself in jail. But this narrow shave by a highly respected corporation left a lasting impression on the boards of corporate America. By law, the directors of a business cannot be held responsible for the share price, since it is the market that decides the price. But in today's materialistic society, the owners of the company seem interested only in the price of their stock and will sell out if it does not rise fast enough. The days of responsible ownership seem to be a long, long time ago. The directors of businesses would not be human if they did not adapt to this constant threat, and their response was a spate of friendly defensive mergers to put the capital value of the merged corporations so high as to put the new conglomerate out of range of most bidders. But to make this assurance doubly sure, there was also a trend to concentrate on short-term profits to raise the earnings per share, even if this did damage to the long-term development of the business.

THE FREE MARKET MODEL

Despite the speculative froth, the free market model has continued to work. It was the centrally controlled economies that collapsed. And yet, the free market model is not without its flaws. During the Cold War, we had to defend free markets for so long and so strongly that we were reluctant to admit that our own system had its flaws. We saw the free market as part of our democratic freedom, and it followed that free markets should have as few restraints as possible. But Christians are wary, believing that no system, however good, can stay uncorrupted. The Bible has warnings and safeguards against economic power. We must always remember its warnings and ask who benefits from the freedom to do as they like, and who, if there are no safeguards, will suffer.

Although the economic background to Bible times was very

different from our own industrial society, the Bible does lay down some quite sharp guidelines regarding economic activity. The laws were clearly aimed to pass down the capital (the land) of each family intact from generation to generation, and the laws were totally opposed to the accumulation of that capital by the rich and powerful. The legal instrument was the Law of Jubilee. Every fifty years, the family farm had to go back to its original owners, and the debts run up in hard times had to be canceled. Land was the capital of an agricultural society, and the rich were not free to corner it, adding "house to house and . . . field to field."

So the biblical model was family capitalism. The family's independence was to be protected against the state. Naboth was entitled to oppose King Ahab's demand for his vineyard, and God punished Ahab for seizing it. Other prophets attacked the rich for using their wealth to buy off the judges and rulers. Moving to the New Testament, we find James telling Christians not to give undue deference to the rich, for "Is it not the rich who are exploiting you? Are they not the ones who are dragging you into court?" (James 2:6).

Nowhere in Christian Scriptures, Old Testament or New, is there any support for an open-ended capitalist system in which the rich get richer while the poor get poorer. The ideal is a society in which each family is under its own vine and its own fig tree (1 Kings 4:25; Mic. 4:4; Zech. 3:10). Any system should be judged by its results. Is it fair between citizens? Does it give equality of opportunity to earn a living? Does it protect us against exploitation by the rich and powerful?

CONSUMER PROTECTION

One of the greatest protections for the consumer is the ability to choose not just what to buy but also from whom to buy it; so we are protected by laws that encourage competition. It is in the country's interest to see that the products with best value-for-money succeed. No one has a right to stay in business. If someone finds a better product or a cheaper way of making it, then the old must match it or go.

But the more complex the products we buy, the more food that comes to us in cans and in highly processed form, the more we need consumer protection. It is not just a matter of making sure that the weights and measures are accurate; it is also that the contents of the cans are safe, that the electrical products will not kill us, that the tires on our automobiles will not blow out, that the signaling on our railroads works, and that our airplanes do not fall out of the sky.

Just how complex all these laws are, we in the European Union found out when we had to bring all national laws in line for the single European market. Each country suddenly found that its standards of safety had to be altered—always, of course, to make products safer. The biggest outcry was from the small brewers in South Germany. Their special beers were, they said, part of their way of life and not to be altered by bureaucrats. But somehow even that problem found a solution.

Often the manufacturers welcome the standards. When the managers at Goodyear Tire in Wolverhampton went to the local pub, they were always tempted to go around the parking lot to see whether there were any tires with less than the legal depth of tread. Tough standards were good business.

Flaws in the Capital Market

When I was CEO of a construction company, I had my first experience of a hostile bid. They were a rarity at the time, and there was little to guide us on how to counter it. I had noticed that one shareholder had 17 percent of the voting shares, and the friendly institutional holdings plus the board did not hold all that many more. We could only be weeks away from a bid, and for those weeks we thought of nothing else but the actions needed to get the share price to reflect the real worth of the company. We announced the much needed revaluation of a huge apartment block, bought out our partners in a very profitable company, and consolidated its profits with ours and paid for the purchase by a private issue of shares to institutional holders. Profits were looking good, so we also forecast the coming rise. All of this raised the share price, the cost of buying control became too great, and the buyers sold their shares for a large profit. But the market had established the proper price for the shares, as only a competitive market can.

Three years later I saw the other side of the coin. The London market had its first really big hostile bid, bitterly fought between two American bidders, for the British Aluminum Company. Alcoa was bidding for a major stake; Reynolds Metals, with Tube Investments (TI), a British company, was bidding for a complete takeover. The share price soared and Reynolds and TI won.

After seven interviews, an intelligence test, and a report on my handwriting, I was offered the job of CEO of the British Aluminum Company under its new owners. The defense of a free market, which allows hostile bids, is that the bidders can make better use of the assets. So, on arrival, I asked for the calculations backing the bid price. If there were better ways to run the company, I needed to know what they were. I found that there were no such calculations and asked what had decided the price. The cynical reply was, "The heat of the chase!"

The bid was made at the end of a long boom in the industry, where the main problem was to find capacity to meet the demand, and British Aluminum had a big new smelter coming on production. But from the time of the takeover, the price of aluminum dropped swiftly and steadily. I was saved by having the wisest and most understanding chairman, who had joined just ahead of me, and together we took a series of tough decisions that saw us through—but not to a future that ever justified the bid price.

Four years later, the company loaned me to the British government. By that time, takeover bids and mergers had become a fashion, and I asked for some work to be done on their economic effectiveness. The answer, which did not surprise me, was that there was no evidence of the synergy that was supposed to come from mergers. The other conclusion, not surprising when we look back, was that mergers were defensive, aiming to produce a market capitalization that would put the merged conglomerate out of reach of a hostile bid.

BOOM AND SLUMP

Our conclusions made no difference to the conglomerate boom, which had a life of its own. George Soros, in his explanation of the boom, says,

> [E]arnings growth . . . loomed larger in the investors' minds than other so-called fundamentals, such as dividends or balance sheets, and investors were not terribly discriminating about the way per-share earnings growth was achieved. Certain companies managed to exploit this bias. . . . They decided to . . . acquire other companies whose stock was selling at a lower multiple of earnings resulting in higher earnings per share [for the acquiring company]. Investors appreciated the earnings growth and accorded high multiples to the shares, which enabled the conglomerates to continue the process (*The Crisis of Global Capitalism* [New York: Public Affairs, 1998], 50).

This mushroom growth depended on the market's ignoring the flaw in the method of valuation, and was sustained by pure greed. The moment of truth comes when the boom turns down and some of the conglomerate's acquisitions start to make losses in businesses about which the top management knows nothing. In America, Soros says,

> The climactic event was the attempt by Paul Steinberg to acquire the Chemical Bank: It was fought and defeated by the establishment.
>
> When stock prices began to fall, the decline fed on itself . . . and many of the high-flying conglomerates literally disintegrated (*Crisis,* 51).

Soros was illustrating a central argument in his book *The Crisis of Global Capitalism.* He says that, contrary to monetarist theory, stock markets and currency markets do not produce equilibrium. He argues that yesterday's view of the market, as recorded in the Wall Street prices, is unstable, because it is immediately changed by those who react to it. In the boom, the rise in the market was continually reinforced by the greed of those who wanted to climb aboard; and the slump that followed was reinforced by the fear of those who wanted to get out.

The proper social function of the stock market is to provide investors with liquidity, which is easy access to their savings when they need them. The proper economic function of the market is to channel funds to the corporations which have the best record of using them well. Stock market booms and slumps are destabilizing to both of these proper functions.

The moving force of a stock market boom is plain greed, which, even if it recognizes the risks, sustains itself in the hope that the stock can be sold before the downturn comes. It has hardly anything to do with professional assessment of the long-term value of the stock traded.

From the eighteenth-century Dutch tulip boom and South Sea Bubble to the dot.com boom of the twenty-first century, there is always a plausible story line. Sarah, formidable widow of the first

Duke of Marlborough, who defeated the tyrannical Louis XIV, summoned her financial advisers to know why they had invested her money in the South Sea Company. When they told her the story line, she said, "The thing is ridiculous," and ordered them to sell all her stock at once. As a result of her shrewd common sense, her descendants live in Blenheim Palace to this day.

The Duchess had only her common sense to pit against the experts. Today we should know a whole lot better, but that does not seem to stop the folly. When I was chair of a lumber company, a well-known tea merchant offered a high price for our shares. They knew nothing about lumber. So we explained to them that the world market price was going down and that our profits would soon be cut sharply. But if they insisted, we would tell shareholders that the bid was well over the true value. They ignored our warning and our shareholders took their money. The profits of their new acquisition dropped sharply, as we had predicted, and helped to reduce the owner's profits and their share price. That made them vulnerable to takeover by a giant international food company. Guessing that the food giant was not really interested in sawmills and knew nothing about the price of Canadian and Russian lumber, the lumber company management found the finance for a buyout and the company continues to flourish—as, of course, did the brokers who put through all the deals!

BUSINESS NEEDS MORAL MOORINGS

I felt at the time that business had gotten loose from its moral moorings. Our legal duty was to our shareholders, and we had to recommend the high bid. But what of all the people who worked for the company? The new owners knew nothing of the business, and the shares were just financial counters. What entitled the new owners to play with the careers of the managers and to risk the jobs of the workers in the sawmills? Surely ownership should carry

some broader responsibilities. In that case the management buyout solved the problem, melding management and ownership, and
gave those who ran the company the old legitimacy of the owner-
manager.

But no one seems to worry any longer about the legitimacy of
management. Those on the payroll worry about the next paycheck,
and the legal owners do not want to look at anything except the
quarterly rise in the earnings per share. And boards of directors
know that there are all kinds of bogus ways of showing a firm quarterly rise. They also know that, if they fail, there will be an early
offer from bidders who will claim that they know how to succeed.

But in real life, away from the froth of the market, most of the
corporations, on which the prosperity of our countries depends,
have to make long-term investment. Research into new processes
and their development into new, saleable products take money and
time. Lead times for the products needed to compete in the
national and international markets take three to four years—maybe
longer—before payoff. And, all that time, the mounting interest
will cut current profits. The real test of professional management
is its ability to hold and increase its market share. And if the owners of the stock insist on selling out on the short-term dips in profit
caused by long-term investment, then they undermine our whole
industrial system.

As we saw in chapter 2, this insistence on the short term can
make management cynical. It can say that, if the owners are only
interested in the short term, management will give it them. Then
they award themselves "golden parachutes," so that when the
short term fails and there is a hostile bid, they will be protected
financially. Or they can look for a friendly bidder, who will keep
them on or pay them off handsomely. Meanwhile, they sit on each
other's boards for mutual support.

INSTITUTIONAL SHAREHOLDERS AND BANKS

For the large institutional shareholders, who have major stakes in every large corporation, none of this short-termism seems to make any sense.

I asked the managers of one of Britain's major life insurance companies why they took so much notice of quarterly earnings per share. Their own liabilities were long-term; surely it was the long-term performance of their investments that mattered? They said that they relied for their new business on the brokers, who were mainly interested in the quarterly performance of their portfolio against that of other life insurance companies. So I asked a Christian friend who was a broker, why he was so interested in the short-term performance of the life insurance company portfolios he sold. He said that his clients checked them out, and if they found that he had sold them a policy in a company with poor short-term performance, regardless of its good long-term record, he could be sued for bad advice.

The other big providers of finance are the major deposit banks. Banks have to match their short-term deposits by short-term loans. But the direction of bank loans is still a major influence on the way the whole economy moves. In Germany, the banks have big long-term stakes in their country's major corporations, and they have seats, with the trade union representatives, on the supervisory boards of those corporations. But in the Anglo-American structure, the banks do not have the long-term commitment that these board seats give. So they are free to swing their priorities to finance whatever is in fashion.

In the 1970s, the British banks fueled a great property boom. I was back from public service and, once more, CEO of a large construction company with a major property development division and a big property portfolio. The government had just released the banks from their credit ceilings and they were able to put much more out on loan. Government had hoped that it would go into export industry to help the country's trade balance, but the immediate demand was for loans for property development. So the big four deposit banks started lending money to new secondary banks, who lent it on to property developers, who got to work as if there were no tomorrow. We had to decide whether to follow.

Property values depend on future rents, which, in turn, depend on future demand, so we only had to extrapolate our own in-house figures to know that the new values were way over the top. Then our building division asked what we were going to do for a second office block for our property division, where they had built the first block and laid the foundations for both. We asked for the square footage of the offices currently under construction in the city and divided it by the annual occupation of new office space. That showed that it would take eight years to fill the offices currently under construction. So we decided not to put up the second building and avoided the financial catastrophe that overtook those developers who had gone with the trend.

It is not easy for a CEO to advise the board to go in one direction when all the major banks in the country are going the other way. So it is the kind of crisis that fixes it in your mind for all time that bankers have no special wisdom and are just as likely to follow the crowd as anyone else. Many developers went bankrupt in the "bust" that followed, and the secondary banks would have followed them into oblivion but for a government "lifeboat" that helped to rescue them. The prime minister, Edward Heath, complained that he gave the markets freedom and all he got was a property boom.

MARKET FUNDAMENTALISM

But that was only a beginning. By the early 1980s, "market fundamentalism" had taken over in both the United Kingdom and the

United States. Both countries financed their expansion by running huge external trade deficits. The United Kingdom's did not show for the first few years of North Sea oil production, but, apart from the short-lived oil bonanza, external trade was in deep deficit. In ten years the United States was turned, as we've noted earlier, from the world's biggest creditor into its biggest debtor.

The second oil shock, in 1980, produced a huge cash surplus in oil-producing countries with tiny populations—a surplus that they could not possibly use for their own economy. They deposited it with Western banks, who lent it to developing countries. They in turn used a good part of it for investment in exports to the West. But the oil shock had brought Western expansion to a halt, so the markets on which the new investment depended dried up, and many countries, especially in South America, could neither service the loans nor repay them.

A focused development, using one of the international institutions, would have put the money where it provided the quickest turnaround for the Western economies, on whose growth the developing world depends for its exports. But the banks somehow lost sight of the tough notion that freedom implies responsibility and still expected a government bailout for their bad debts.

PLAIN GREED

The 1990s seemed to be a time of highly successful long-term growth without any of the boom and bust of the two decades before. The problem is that human greed has not gone away. A fair return for our investment is not greed. Greed is playing the market, hunched over our PC, following the movement of the stocks day by day and maybe hour by hour, just like the gambler who feels that, if he goes out to relieve himself, he may miss the winning break. Greed is wanting far more money than we need and taking needless risks to get it. Greed is what produces the mindless scramble of the boom and the desperate rush of the bust. The spectacular disasters of 2002 and the midsummer slump of share prices show that none of this has gone away.

Greed leads not just individuals but even national governments to take foolish and dangerous risks. When World War I came to an end, the European allies wanted to get every cent out of Germany in "reparations" for her aggression. The new democratic German government was made to sign the Versailles Treaty. But Germany was broke and could not pay. Worse, a great and proud nation was humiliated. The greedy allies did not get their money; they got Hitler and World War II instead.

After World War II, America was in a far better position to dictate the terms of the settlement and, with Canada, set up the Marshall Plan, which put a ruined continent back on its feet. That generosity included not only their allies but their former enemies, Austria, Finland, Italy, and Germany. Separately, they put Japan, too, back on its feet. Their generosity gave the West half a century of peace and was a standing answer to communist propaganda.

But as we have seen, by the end of the Cold War in 1990, that spirit of generosity seemed to have withered. Democracy had taken over in Moscow and Kiev, but both Russia and Ukraine were broke. Half of the workforce in the major cities had been making armaments, which the other half of their economy could no longer pay for. To keep this huge unemployed workforce fed, the two governments had to inflate their currency. But the West, represented by the Group of Seven (the United States, Canada, Germany, the United Kingdom, France, Italy, and Japan, plus the president of the European Commission, standing in for the remaining members of the European Union) would not give more than an unconditional offer of $1.5 billion in aid until inflation was brought under control—in which case they would receive a total of $5 billion. It was a real "Catch 22," because the

Russians and Ukrainians could not bring inflation under control without money to feed starving workers. Even had they been able to do so, only $5 billion was promised, when the unofficial report from the World Bank was that Russia alone needed a minimum of $15 billion.

I was responsible for the European Parliament's report on aid to Eastern Europe, and we had hearings, to which we asked members of the new Russian Parliament as well as their government. The Russian Parliament did not think that the financial reforms would work without much higher aid, though their government, anxious to keep its goodwill, went along with the West. The European Parliament voted unanimously (a very rare event) for a more generous treatment of Eastern Europe, but the G-7 would not budge.

Since NATO countries were still spending $150 billion a year on research, development, and production of Cold War weaponry, we had further hearings and made a second proposal. We suggested that, within their defense budget, NATO countries convert part of their arms production to the manufacture of the equipment Russia and Ukraine would need to develop their enormous natural resources, earn a trade surplus, and get their people back to work. The new Western equipment would convert the Russian and Ukrainian arms industries to civil manufacture. So, with conversion of arms plants West and East, there would be a mutual force reduction, which would make the world a safer place. We proposed that the program should be under the same strict conditions as the Marshall Plan. This would give the West the leverage it needed to insist on a workable and enforceable commercial law and a Western-style, publicly accountable banking system.

At another hearing, members of the Western defense industry said that the conversion was feasible and, since it would open up new Russian and Ukrainian markets, desirable. I also had an unforgettable meeting in Moscow with the chiefs of the Russian arms industry, who very reluctantly admitted that they could not do it themselves and believed that, if they had the funds, they could and should convert their plants to civil use. Otherwise, they thought, they would not keep their best technologists in the country.

Before leaving Moscow, the European Union ambassador took me with him on a visit to the board of MiG, the aircraft maker, who had asked to see him. They complained bitterly that, though, with European Union help, they had a contract for tail fins with the French aircraft maker Dassault, and though they could, of course, both make and test tail fins, the test rigs had to be to Western specifications. But a new Western test rig cost money and they had none, nor did Russian banks. What did we expect them to do? Were we playing games with them or were we serious?

Afterwards, two old veterans showed us with great pride around their small museum. It had photographs of the pilots and planes that had shot the Nazi Luftwaffe out of the sky, giving the Allies dominance in the air for the Normandy landing. Not far away was a pillar by the side of the road, marking the high tide of the Nazi advance, just a few miles from central Moscow.

Once more we had a hearing in which Western industry confirmed the feasibility of the dual conversion from weapons to the productive equipment that would give Eastern Europe a self-sustaining economy. And once more the Parliament recorded a rare unanimous vote. The British and Canadian governments said that, since America had by far the greatest defense industry, they would have to look to Washington for a lead. I put the case to our summer meeting with the Congress delegation. They were supportive, since it would help all the districts heavily dependent on defense production; but they pointed out that Congress was reactive—it would need an initiative from the president. I also saw

Senator Sam Nunn, who then chaired the Senate Armed Services Committee. He was extremely sympathetic (he had made a very small initiative in that direction with Senator Richard Lugar) but also said that they would need a proposal from the president. Finally I found myself in the offices of the National Security Council, looking down on the executive suite of the White House. They said that they found the president always open to new ideas.

Whatever President Clinton's faults, the one skill no one denied him was a deep understanding of what would and would not have the support of the American people. What became crystal clear was his belief that the American people did not want the "peace dividend" of lower defense expenditure to be diverted to help the losers of the Cold War, but that they wanted it for themselves. The huge generosity to defeated enemies of two generations ago had withered away in a country now three times as rich. The European members of the G-7, who had been rescued by the Marshall Plan, had even less excuse for such greed.

We have not yet seen all the consequences of this failure by the West to help the former Soviet Union. The Russian "reformers" have gone, the remaining assets of Russian corporations have been taken over by the bosses, and a large part of their foreign earnings has been creamed off into foreign bank accounts. The mafia hired to protect this new wealth are now more powerful than the underpaid police, and there is not enough money to see to the safety of nuclear power stations or to dismantle safely the nuclear submarines.

The Russian defense industry finds business where it can and provides weapons for everyone around the world who wants to shoot their neighbors. "Rogue states" are only dangerous if they can lay hands on the weapons. And no one knows yet whether the Russian president who has inherited this mess will stay a newborn democrat or whether the chaos and poverty in his country will drive him back to the tough and ruthless school in which he was trained. Meanwhile, the 1990s saw Western prosperity at new heights, and the ICBMs are still in their Siberian silos, still pointing at their targets in our own countries. And the result of our greed is that we are now looking at a vast increase in defense spending to build an improbable antimissile system that, even if it works, will not be ready to protect us for years.

Our Markets Are Vulnerable

Successive tariff reductions have increased world trade through greater specialization as export companies concentrate on products at which they excel and the higher export sales enable them to drop less profitable products. That means that even America is more and more dependent on imports. With this increase in world trade has also come a great increase in currency trading, circling around the three major currencies—the U.S. dollar, the euro, and the yen—which can all swing against each other dramatically and unpredictably. Combined with the massive flows of new investment to the Pacific rim, this currency instability produced the Asian crisis of 1997. We had been told not to worry because traders could be protected by "hedge funds," which carried the risk; but in the crisis, the biggest hedge fund went broke.

The problem of global capitalism is the tendency, while all is going well, of peripheral countries like those on the Pacific rim to attract huge loans from Western banks, which then, in a crisis, join the rush to get their money out. To quote Soros again, "The panic was spread [from Thailand] to neighbouring countries by the financial market. I use the image of the wrecking ball, others have referred to the financial contagion as a modern version of the bubonic plague."

When the United States was self-sufficient, the value of the dollar in world currency markets did not matter much. But with the growth of world trade, its value matters a great deal more. While there was no other plausible reserve currency for the rest of the world, it was easy for the United States to borrow billions of dollars a week to fund its foreign trade deficit. But there is now another plausible currency, the euro, backed by eleven countries with a population just under that of the United States and with its own central bank responsible for fixing the rate of interest. The euro's long-heralded arrival was met with some scorn. How can you have a currency without a government?

It was argued against the credibility of the euro that there were still too many employment restrictions on the "Rhine model" economies of the Euro-zone. If they did not loosen up and allow the market to dominate, they would never catch up. But this ignores the steady competitive success of the Euro-zone, which consistently exports more than it imports. The United States, by contrast, which has only achieved its higher growth by running a large trade deficit, now has to compete for the money to fund the deficit at over $1 billion a day.

The euro is unlikely to go away. Britain has so far stayed out and finds, to its cost, that a single market needs a single currency. Britain's farmers were bankrupted when the euro fell by 25 percent against the pound and there was no way that the cost of beef, lamb, or butter could be reduced by 25 percent. The country's three largest automobile plants have been cut to less than a quarter of their normal production. Its largest single steel plant has just closed. It will soon be clear, even to we proud Brits, that a single market needs a single currency, and that just such a currency is here to stay.

The possession of the only major reserve currency in the world protected the United States from the economic problems faced by other countries. But as this book goes to press, the foreign investment in the United States, which offset the huge trade deficit, looks likely to dry up. When the ability to borrow their way out of trouble disappears, countries have to attend to all the problems that they have so far been able to ignore. I found, in the public service in a smaller country, that the first rule is that the world does not owe you a living. Independence comes from selling more than you buy, so that you do not have to borrow. It comes when those with money save more than they spend, so that there is an internal surplus to invest in productive business. It comes when government can raise taxes to cover necessary spending. And all that sounds a lot like the beliefs of the founding fathers who built up America's capital in the first place. It does not sound like the hedonistic society we have now, that spends because it believes, "Eat, drink, and be merry, for tomorrow we die."

7

THE GLOBAL ECONOMY

*"Globalisation is clearly increasing personal economic
and financial risks and reducing the capacity of institutions
to protect individuals."*

ECONOMIC JOURNALIST DIANE COYLE

*"The greatest danger to the United States in the years to come
might well be the large and growing deficit in the
international trade balance."*

NOBEL PRIZE WINNERS
FRANCO MODIGLIANI AND ROBERT M. SOLOW

If rising trade in our own country makes us more prosperous, shouldn't rising global trade do the same for all who join in? So why the riots against "globalization"?

Seattle is one of the most beautiful cities of the United States and, though it has its share of drugs and crime, one of the least troubled. But in 1999 it had its first major riot. The city was hosting the first meeting of the World Trade Organization (WTO), a more inclusive successor to the postwar GATT. Trade is a subject that seldom excites politicians, let alone provokes a riot.

The International Monetary Fund (IMF) has been criticized

for its meanness, and the World Bank for the failure of its aid to end poverty. But there had never been much criticism of GATT's promotion of freer trade. If GATT had a fault, it was that it depended too heavily on the initiative and agreement of the major trading powers, the United States and the European Union. But the new WTO, whose meeting provoked the riot, was set up to deal with that very fault.

GLOBAL TRADE

The steady growth of world trade in the half century since World War II has been the dynamic of the world economy and has been of enormous help to the development of poorer countries. A good price for copper matters far more to Zambia than does aid from the wealthier nations. And the price of the developing world's other primary products also depends heavily on the growth rate of the world economy. Just as important, the reduction of trade barriers by the main industrial countries gives the developing countries better access for their manufactured exports.

In a group of eighteen developing countries that became much more open to international trade after 1980, growth rates have risen from 1.5 percent in the 1960s and 70s to nearly 3 percent in the 1980s and over 5 percent in the 90s. These countries include India, Bangladesh, and China in Asia, and Uganda and Ghana in sub-Saharan Africa. The growth of other developing countries, that did not (for various reasons) open their markets, was near zero in both the 1980s and 90s. Before that, most ex-colonial and communist governments wanted to sell their crops or raw material and did not want to spend these hard-currency earnings on imports. But their local manufactured products were high-cost and poor quality, so they began to want Western consumer goods as much as the West wanted to sell them. Western governments believed that if these countries lowered their trade barriers which protected their local industries, Western imports would set high standards and that would be enough to improve the performance of the local industries so that they could also export to Western markets. The West would produce high-technology and high-investment products and the developing world would produce those where cheap labor had the advantage.

So, if the liberalization of international trade is so helpful, and if organizations such as the WTO exist to protect local industries, why were there protests, first in Seattle in 1999, then in Prague, and again at the World Economic Forum in Davos, Switzerland, and at Quebec in 2001?

One clue is the slowdown in the West to no more than 2 percent growth, so that competition from the imports of low-wage countries has begun to hurt. There was strong representation in the Seattle protests from the labor unions, one of whose leaders complained that the global market was like "an economic Wild West," a system for which there were a hundred different rules of law, which are much discussed, while the might of raw economic power prevails. The constant fear of American labor leaders is the cheap labor of the millions of workers in poor countries and its power to undercut American industry in products in which little capital is needed and labor is a high proportion of the cost.

Overall American employment figures are high, because, overall, new jobs have replaced those that have been lost. But the small town that has lost its main employer is not helped by a whole lot of new jobs in a big city several hundred miles away. The process is disruptive of families and communities and, as it goes on, leaves an increasing number of people with a grudge against "the system." Though the majority have benefited from recent economic growth, there is a very large group of dispossessed, and even those who right now wonder when their turn will come.

The United States has a long-standing reputation for taking

risks for growth. A hundred years ago the slogan was "Go west, young man." There were always opportunities somewhere for those with the "get up and go." A nation of immigrants did not seem to mind where they were, so long as there was a job worth doing. My immigrant Uncle Fred's first job in 1907 was selling Persian carpets in a big store in Philadelphia. He moved on to mining in Idaho and, before his accidental death, wrote home that he intended to move on again to real estate in California. That mood of open opportunity was hit by the Great Depression of 1929–1932 but came again with the prolonged postwar boom.

Although New England lost its textile industry, that industry was smartly replaced by the first wave of high-tech companies. But the optimistic mood seems to be changing again. America's flagship automobile industry has lost heavily to Japan and Europe, and many fear that *their* industry will be next. And much of the new employment is in low-paid, insecure service jobs rather than in the long-term skilled jobs in manufacturing that had given America its dominance in export markets.

AMERICA'S SOARING TRADE DEFICIT

In the 1990s, much of the growth in demand was met by imports, bringing a steadily rising U.S. trade deficit, now running at over $400 billion a year. So the years of expanding consumption have not helped the long-term job market in the United States. Worse, the increasing need to borrow to fund the currency deficit has kept U.S. interest rates relatively high, pushed the dollar to an uncompetitive level, and raised the cost of the investment needed to reverse the trend. Small wonder that the labor unions took to the streets in Seattle. It is not hard for Americans, living in a continental economy, with a tradition of self-sufficiency, to believe that a strong dollar is good for America and a sign of the country's strength. But America is no longer self-sufficient and exports no longer pay for imports.

The United States has to borrow over a billion dollars a day to find the currency needed to pay for the excess of imports (including oil) over exports, and that is a weakness, not a strength. To meet that gap, the interest paid on dollar bonds has to be higher than the rate paid by a currency in surplus. It is that premium that pushes up the value of the dollar in currency markets. That higher price makes it harder for American exports to compete in world markets and makes imports to America cheaper than home-produced goods. So the labor leaders complain that their members are losing their jobs, and they put the blame on foreign imports.

America is not alone in this fix. Britain suffered the same over-valued currency, the same high interest rates, the same lack of investment, and the same growing trade deficit. Continental Europe, with its balanced trade, sees it as a fault of the "Anglo-Saxon" system and believes its own way is best. In Britain, the political reaction to this situation is a rise in nationalist, anti-European feeling, and a wrong-headed determination not to exchange the overvalued pound for the new and more competitive European currency.

A major cut in American taxes would increase consumption but it would send the present record deficit even higher. The risk is that, even without a tax cut, the flow of yen and euros to fund the American deficit will suddenly dry up. To quote from Modigliani and Solow:

> Creditors may decide that they are not able to finance a country's growing debt for fear of a depreciation of the debtor's currency that lowers asset values in their own currencies. If such a thing happened to the United States, there could be very unpleasant consequences for Americans. The size and power of the American economy have protected it from capital flight . . . but there is no guarantee that this will remain true. Nor could the dollar be propped up by the Fed or the Treasury, since their reserves are $60 billion compared with a foreign trade deficit of

$400 billion a year, just two months borrowing (*New York Times,* April 10, 2001).

Just over a year later, it looks as if that moment of truth has come and, already, in protecting U.S. steel companies from imports, it looks as if the president is not too worried about the promotion of international trade. So it would not be surprising if U.S. labor leaders also felt that the time had come to stop the trend toward open international markets. It would be even less surprising if we look at the WTO's next agenda item, the admission of China's 1.2 billion people to the world trading system, including the American market.

FREE TRADE WITH CHINA?

Overseas Chinese already dominate the trade of Southeast Asia. Hong Kong and Taiwan are all Chinese. Singapore has a dominant Chinese majority. The merchant class of Malaysia is Chinese and they also do most of the trade in Indonesia. What is to stop the mainland Chinese from swamping Western markets once they have a foothold?

The answer may be that the expatriate Chinese, who have done so well in Southeast Asia, are the limited elite who had the ability and vision to get out of the communist state and start on their own. Maybe the hundreds of millions brought up under communism are unlikely for a long time, even if they have the education, to turn into sharp merchants and business leaders. And if they do, maybe they will create wealth for us as well as for themselves. But if we were labor leaders, we might be inclined to put a shot across the bow of the new World Trade Organization before it could take China on board.

They might also believe that their shot would be the more powerful if there were some other shots too.

DESTROYING THE WORLD'S NATURAL RESOURCES

One shot of protest is against the devastation by industry of the earth's natural resources and its natural habitat. Action has been made more urgent by the warnings of global warming. The protestors' case is that the clear-cutting of vast forests and the prolific use of fossil fuel will bring an irreversible natural catastrophe in our lifetime. So the ecologists are out there with the labor unions. Christians who believe that God has made us trustees of the world's resources for generations to come must also protest. It is our job to leave the world a better place than we found it, not to deplete its God-given resources.

On the other hand we do not worship nature, like the new pagans. Natural resources are given by a good God for our use. Trees are not sacred. We can clear forests provided we replant what we have cut down. God told Israel to leave the land fallow for a sabbatical year. We should not over-fish and wipe out a whole species. We are entitled to use fossil fuel so long as we leave our children with alternative ways of providing the energy we have used up. There is a lot in the "Green" agenda with which Christians should agree.

GLOBAL CORPORATIONS

Another shot of protest rings out against the power of multinational corporations. The global economy not only trades in goods and services, it also trades in corporations. There has never been such buying and selling across national frontiers. Daimler Benz used to be a flagship German builder of dull, reliable, and prestigious automobiles. From its base in the beautiful South German city of Stuttgart, it outsold its competitors across the world. Then it merged with Chrysler, America's number three automobile company. No one any longer knew who ran what, and the marriage seems a disastrous failure. Ditto the merger of Mercedes' great rival, BMW, with Britain's Rover. Sweden's Saab disappeared inside General Motors, and decisions were taken in Detroit rather than Gothenburg. Behind these deals in the highly visible automobile industry, lots of other trades were going on, leaving employees in the hands of decision makers in faraway places.

Because the plants of multinational corporations tend to be well guarded and their offices anonymous, the only American company visibly present everywhere, and with invitingly breakable windows, is McDonald's. Most unfairly, it takes the brunt of every protest.

THIRD WORLD DEBT

The other major cause of protest, argued soberly and away from the rioters, was a genuine Third World issue: relief from the great burden of debt hanging over so many developing countries. The case for debt relief is overwhelming and has been recognized by the lending governments. Where countries simply do not have the resources to pay, the debt is not a viable asset on anyone's books and should be written off; and there are other debts that should and can be scaled down.

But not all debt failure is faultless. Every aid package has built-in cash-flow projections that allow for repayment. Where the repayments are not made, creditors are entitled to ask what happened to the money. In the case of the late and unlamented president of the Democratic Republic of Congo (formerly Zaire), we know that it went into Swiss bank accounts and high living. In the case of the late and equally unlamented government of Ethiopia, every last cent went into arms. But if the cash flow from the project had been based on careful forecasts, agreed between lender and borrower, but on assumptions that turned out to be mistaken, then the aid agencies should be allowed to make a case for a write-off.

POORER COUNTRIES NEED THE WTO

Unlike government aid, the benefits of free trade go directly into the bank accounts of local businesses and on into the local economy. They are not siphoned off, as aid has been, by corrupt or militaristic governments. So it seems a pity that the WTO, the institution needed to help promote the trade of developing countries, should be the recipient of so much undeserved hostility. True, free trade has not worked so well for all poor countries as it does for all the rich. As the West gets richer, the poorest seem to get poorer. But the WTO is needed to help close that gap.

There are other problems for the WTO to sort out. Western drug companies have spent billions in research. So when a drug works, they charge a price that brings their money back to fund the next expensive research project. That price is too high for poor countries, which are left short of drugs for AIDS and other desperate diseases. South Africa brought a legal case and won a lower price for drugs to deal with AIDS. But that does not solve the problem for other countries and other drugs. The WTO, where rich and poor countries meet as equals, is the right place to formulate an international patents law that will give affordable drugs and still keep the drug companies in business.

FREE TRADE IS AN ALTERNATIVE TO ILLEGAL IMMIGRATION

There is another pressing reason for free trade. If the free trade area with Mexico creates export jobs south of the Rio Grande, and European aid creates them along the North African coast, there will be fewer illegal immigrants trying to enter the United States and the European Union. Instead of forcing the West to slam the door against illegal immigrants in search of work, it creates the employment right where the workers are and gives poor countries the chance to pull themselves up by their own bootstraps.

BUT MORE THAN FREE TRADE IS NEEDED
TO GIVE POORER COUNTRIES LIFTOFF

The industrial and commercial machine of the West has swift reflexes. It can adapt quickly to changes in the market. If one product becomes obsolete, then another takes its place. If a whole industry becomes obsolete, another soon springs up to take over. Capital markets, corporate management, and merchants take change in stride. It is not enough, however, as we have seen in Eastern Europe, to change from state control to the market economy. The free market needs competent and trained management, the rule of law, solvent banks, a stable currency, and honest officials.

Nor is aid money, alone, enough. Forty and more years since political independence, forty years and more of international aid, yet there is little sign of any breakthrough by the poorer countries. Output and wages are still stuck at about a tenth of that paid in the West. Some countries are sunk in chronic poverty.

The big success story is East Asia. I once arrived in Korea representing British exporters and was given an "over the top" welcome by the chairman of one of Korea's largest companies. I asked our ambassador the reason for the extravagant treatment. He said that our export credits financed the Korean man's start-up, one of our own companies taught him the business, his low wages enabled him to take over our own export markets—and he was "very grateful."

The other "Asian tigers" are Taiwan, Hong Kong, and Singapore. Malaysia, with its strong Chinese minority, has made great advances too. Though they were all involved in the crash of 1997–1998, they had built the commercial structure needed to pick themselves up again. And, no doubt, China is building some of that structure too. But elsewhere there is still abject poverty.

THE BIGGEST SINGLE PROBLEM IN DEVELOPING NATIONS IS THE STRANGLEHOLD OF FINANCIAL CORRUPTION

We have looked at the result of some breakdown of trust in the West, but elsewhere in the world the stranglehold of corruption is lethal. In most of Asia and Africa, merchants seem to trust only their own families and Western multinationals. There are few local public corporations of any size.

The grip of corruption in some countries is deadening, for the reasons we explored in chapter 5. The immediate effect of corruption is to divert funds on a massive scale from the poor to the rich. The bribes, which are paid to a bank outside the country, are added to the cost of the contract; even if the contract goes ahead, there will be fewer roads, fewer houses or hospital beds, fewer start-up plants.

More important, Western business does not see why it should be entangled in a country with endemic corruption. There is little attraction in trading with a country with poor infrastructure, minimal local markets, and low skills. Without the web of corruption, all that might be put right. But the web of corruption is a decisive deterrent.

When the issue was coming to a head in the 1970s, I sat next to the chairman of one of the major U.S. electronics companies at a lunch. He said, "I don't care how much business I lose, I am not going to be called down to Washington to appear before a congressional committee on charges of bribery." He knew that his most precious asset was his personal reputation. If that were ruined, he would never hold another job. Another U.S. company issued a brisk directive to all their overseas staff: "No extra-contractual payments are to be made by anyone, to anyone, for any reason, at any time."

At the Davos Management Forum (now renamed, more grandly, the World Economic Forum), I spoke two years running on business ethics, and the burning issue was what to do about demands for bribes. A world-famous international chemical company was thinking of building a refinery in an Asian country, but the demand for bribes bothered them. I said that it was a useful warning. Once their company had built the refinery, they could be held to ransom. There were other countries nearby that did not demand bribes; why choose a country that did?

From Davos I went to Zurich to call in on one of the three major Swiss banks to protest their acceptance of deposits from corrupt payments. Their reply was that they could not possibly ask a client where his money had come from. Since then the world has become littered with safe havens for laundered money, pinpoints on the map dependent on the protection of the West but carelessly undermining the integrity and trust on which its economic health depends.

The steady miring of developing countries in corruption has offset the efforts of the West to help through development projects. In a vigorous discussion recently with church leaders in an African capital, I argued that their country's future depended on the very strong and influential Christian community. They should set Christian standards, as generations before them had done in conditions just as tough. They said that they could do nothing until the West forgave the debts. My wife talked to the women, who had far more initiative and were dealing with the problem of poverty by teaching women how to manage their plots of land and develop markets for their produce.

FREE TRADE HELPS THIRD WORLD CHRISTIANS ESCAPE THE BLIGHT OF CORRUPTION

In most countries in sub-Saharan Africa, the Christian church is twice as strong as it is now in the West. As the countries of the West pulled themselves up by their own bootstraps because of their strong Christian ethic, so democratic countries like Nigeria, Uganda, Kenya, and others should be able to do the same; and access to Western markets could be decisive. That is a continuing strong argument for free international trade.

Access to Western markets helps Christians even in countries where they are a small minority. A young Christian engineer in a southern Asian country was a partner in his father's electronics business. His father insisted that bribery was the custom of the country, but he replied that, as a Christian, he could not give bribes. So they split the business and he concentrated on export markets, which, though more competitive, were free of bribery. Because his export business brought in much needed hard currency, he was not pressed for bribes by officials at home and, fairly soon, his business far outstripped that of his father.

There is a wider role model for Christians in corrupt countries. The seventeenth-century French Protestants, the Huguenots, set up not only their own manufacturing businesses but also their own overseas trading network, backed by their own bankers. Their markets were the nearby Protestant countries of Switzerland, Holland, northern Germany, and Britain. Louis XIV's minister of commerce, Jean Baptiste Colbert, asked what he could do for these dynamic exporters. They said simply, "Laissez faire et laissez passer," or "Just let us get on with it and let our goods through." When, in his folly, Louis XIV made life in France impossible for the Huguenots, they still had their customers and their own finance, so they took their manufacturing skills over to their customers' countries, adding a decisive extra boost to the economic growth of Prussia, Holland, and Britain, and to the new colonists in North America, while, as we have noted, France went into long-term decline.

The success of Singapore and Hong Kong must owe something to the strength of the Christian churches there, allied to the old established commercial expertise of the Chinese; and the Christian church in prosperous South Korea has grown rapidly in one generation. The growing Christian churches in Africa, Eastern Europe, and South America still have to establish a rounded Christian way of life that follows the Bible pattern and does not conform to the lifestyle of those around them. The "prosperity gospel," as wrong as it is attractive, especially in poor countries, reflects the greed of a society that wants something for nothing. The hankering after miraculous cures for poverty is nearer to the witch doctor than to the scientific method fostered by the seventeenth-century Reformed church. And the new churches of South America have not yet realized the revolutionary changes that can come from the full impact of Christian standards on their societies.

So, despite the failures to date, the West should try to encourage the growth of industry in poorer countries, and to accept that these countries will make the labor-intensive products, leaving the West to concentrate on its high-tech economy. The challenge to the growing Christian minorities is to provide the culture of trust and professionalism needed to make an industrial economy work, earning hard currency from exports to Western markets.

The Christian faith may be in decline in the West, but it is making great gains in the poorer parts of the world. The most explosive expansion is in China. The African churches are twice as strong and almost totally resistant to secular humanism. In South America, the Catholics are losing but the Protestants are gaining fast. And in the formerly communist countries of Eastern Europe, young shoots of the Christian faith are growing again. In remote Kazakhstan, the church has risen in ten years from almost nothing to an estimated hundred thousand.

Of all the practical help that the West can give to these countries, the most effective in the long run is likely to be on-the-spot training in the professional ethic, with its deep roots in the Christian faith. It is a race against time because, despite the difference in wage costs, Western exports can wipe out employment in whole towns in sub-Saharan Africa. The largest industrial town in Kenya has been badly damaged by Western imports with which it could not compete. That is one reason why aid agencies have swung away from capital investment in the country's public infrastructure and are concentrating more on projects that help privately owned local companies compete effectively by finding the right niche in Western markets.

THE VULNERABILITY OF THE WEST

The riches of the West make us especially vulnerable. Our great increase in consumption makes even the United States, with all its natural resources, dependent on other countries. The nation states of Western Europe recognized this growing dependence by forming the European Union, and no one state can hold the others to ransom. But, on both sides of the Atlantic, the ships that carry our trade are almost all foreign-built and -owned, and those foreign-owned ships also carry most of the fuel that powers our industry and transport and that keeps our homes warm in winter and cool in summer.

Therefore, both rich countries and poor need the rule of law in the global marketplace, and both need the WTO to agree on what the trading laws should be and to make those laws effective. It is hard enough to get global agreement, and those who try to wreck it with their riots should ask who is to gain by rubbishing the only organization capable of making and monitoring the rule of law.

GLOBAL MONEY MARKETS

For most people, money is a mystery. Our main interest is that our savings and our pension funds keep their value. Since history began, kings have devalued their currency by clipping the edges off their coins; and, though most of us don't quite know how, today's money seems to lose its value too. We also read about financial crises, and hope that the chairman of the Fed will protect us from the evils of inflation and another crash. But despite the careful hands of the Fed, we hear about financial crashes in the world out there and wonder whether they will one day come to hurt us too.

For a long time after World War II there was no problem. The mighty dollar ruled, and no other currency could touch it. In the Eisenhower years, all was for the best in the best of all possible worlds. The dollar was fixed to gold, and other currencies were fixed to the dollar. Any country needing support for its currency had to argue their case to the new, postwar International Monetary Fund. Like an old-fashioned grandmother, the IMF said, "Don't do that again," and set the terms and conditions of the loan.

Then the Vietnam War brought unexpected and ever-rising costs. President Johnson did not want to raise taxes to pay for this unpopular expedition, so he borrowed instead. President Nixon, his successor, did the same, until the borrowings reached the point where Nixon had to break the link between the dollar and gold. With that devaluation of the dollar, he removed the cornerstone of the world's currency and ended a quarter century of monetary stability. But the United States was still the world's greatest creditor and, if not the fixed cornerstone, still the steady hinge of its monetary system. Countries needing to devalue against the dollar still had to negotiate conditions with the IMF.

Then came the spending spree of the 1980s and 90s, turning the United States from the world's greatest creditor into its greatest debtor. As the administration trawled the world for cash, it had to pay higher rates of interest, mainly to the Japanese.

The higher interest rates hit Europe hard. To keep its economy going, the European Union abolished all remaining barriers to trade between its member states, and the late 1980s saw a steady increase in employment. Though the deutsche mark was not the dollar, it was the firm hinge of Europe's money. But Europe still lacked the single currency for its single market of 318 million people. Having its own currency would also help Europe set its own interest rates. The euro was conceived in the early 1990s and born at the turn of the millennium. While each member state of the European Union had to use its own currency reserves to protect its currency from waves of speculative selling, they could wake up and find that half of their reserves had gone before breakfast—which happened to Britain and two other countries in 1992. Now the reserves of eleven countries are enough to deal with speculation and, with much of the world's trading done in the two major currencies (the dollar and the euro), the openings for disruptive speculation are much smaller.

Meanwhile, the world's currencies have had a rough ride in the South American crisis of the 1980s, the Mexican crisis of 1994, the "Asian tigers" crisis of 1997, and the Russian loan default of 1998. The last was in many ways the worst, first because it had been a long time since a major country defaulted on its debts, and second because the great hedge fund, Long-Term Capital Management (LTCM), could not meet its huge obligations. Its bankruptcy could have brought down major banks and, as one commentator said, "Global meltdown appeared imminent." Catastrophe was avoided by arm-twisting at the Fed, which persuaded the banks that a bailout of LTCM would cost them a lot less than LTCM's bankruptcy. But that near-calamity finally killed the fallacy that currency fluctuations didn't matter because you could always insure against them with a hedge fund.

Wherever trade is free to flow, money must be able to flow too. It does not just flow to pay for goods delivered; it flows out for new investment and back again with dividends, and the speculative flows are several times greater. In an open world market, no bureaucracy could track all the transactions.

That would not matter if the flows of money were tied to regular commercial transactions. But money-flows tend to be something like ten times the flow of goods. So what force drives these great destabilizing waves of speculative money that slosh around in the world's financial system? Traders flit between yen, euro, and dollar bonds. If the U.S. economy is doing well, the flow will be that way; if the euro economy begins to overtake, the flow will be the other way. Exchange rates fluctuate around the clock, marking the way the money flows in today's volatile global money market. The one thing we can be sure about is that, with no one in charge, this mindless bull in our expensive china shop can do immense damage. Attempts by governments to buy their own currency to stabilize the market only make fortunes for dealers like George Soros. It is only by looking at the reasons for each crisis that we can get the clues as to how to prevent them.

Each of the last series of crises had its own cause. Western banks had over-lent to the Asian tigers, the local Asian banks lent too much to cronies, and when these debts went bad they covered them up until the banks were below their minimum reserves. So, when the pressure was on, they would have gone bankrupt unless bailed out. And too many Western banks had hedged their investments in other currencies with the Long-Term Capital Management Fund, which could not meet their obligations. In the sanctuary at the top of the stairs in the Federal Reserve Bank in Washington, the high priest of money put together a deal that bailed out those banks and, with American banks solvent, the Asian crisis could be ended.

One thing is sure: in dealing with the waves of money washing around the world, countries cannot leave it to the market. Harvard's Jeffery Sachs says that global market capitalism has an inherent tendency to instability. When the bubble burst in Thailand and Malaysia, MIT's Paul Krugman saw it as a conventional banking panic, taking place across borders. Whether it was conventional or a new phenomenon, the recessions in the affected countries started in the financial markets. We may think bankers are mean, but lending money is their business. So, when the Asian tigers were expanding fast, a lot of dollar bank loans went in behind that success. But when they seemed to be in financial difficulties, the money was pulled out even faster than it went in.

That was not the first time for such a scenario. After the second oil shock, the oil states had billions of dollars to invest, and they put most of it in American banks. Since the oil shock had slowed the Western economies, which were the motor of world growth, it would have been wiser to invest in Western industry, to make sure that it could get going again. A lot of the banks' money—maybe most of it—went instead to Latin America, much into investment for export to the West. But since the Western market had slowed, the new investment for export failed and the companies could not repay the loans. The Western bankers were appalled and hoped that their governments would bail them out. But governments are in a dilemma: if they do not support the banks when they are in trouble, they damage the innocent depositor and create a financial crisis; but if they do bail them out, they encourage them to lend money when they shouldn't.

It is part of the work of the IMF to support currencies under pressure. But the present volume of loose money in the international markets is beyond the powers of the IMF to control. More than fifty years since it was set up, the IMF no longer has the resources for such a task, and in our materialistic and self-centered society there are no votes in giving money to the IMF.

THE MULTINATIONALS

The anti-globalization movement is especially hot against multinational corporations. Although most governments around the world do all they can to attract investment by foreign multinational companies, that does not avoid feelings of suspicion and resentment at managements who take their instructions from a distant head office. Most people want bosses who are accountable to local elected politicians.

There is, all the same, fierce competition for investment in one's own nation from foreign multinationals—or as we in Britain call it, "inward investment." When I chaired the British Overseas Trade Board, it was part of my job to help attract such investment. After rather a rough year for the British economy, our queen was due to sail into Philadelphia on the royal yacht, *Britannia,* for the bicentenary of the U.S. constitution. To help make the case for our economic turnaround, someone had the bright idea of borrowing the *Britannia* while the queen was ashore and inviting leading American industrialists and bankers on board for a day's outing. No one turned down the invitation. The corporate jets flew in from as far away as Texas, and the stretch limousines swayed along the uneven track of the New Jersey Navy Yard to the dockside. The brass work on *Britannia* was gleaming, we had a good discussion, and watched the fleet of "tall ships" sail past as we returned— a memorable day. And, as I recall, the inward investment kept on coming and the British economy went ahead as we predicted.

Inward investment brings new technology and new skills and helps a country start new industries. The new production also replaces imports, and that helps the trade balance. Some countries try to insist on substantial local shareholdings in these multinationals. But most multinationals are not prepared to surrender their unique skills if they have to part with a quarter of the profits. Some countries are so eager to attract investment that they offer tax holidays, and the members of the European Union have had to agree not to compete with each other on the size of such tax breaks.

Sadly but understandably, multinationals avoid countries impoverished by corruption and without an effective rule of law. So those nations that need private investment most are those least likely to receive it.

Most multinational investment is in advanced industrial countries with flourishing markets, and it takes its place easily alongside national companies in the same industry and raises a great deal of its capital by local borrowing. The buying and selling of companies and the flow of dividends back home do add something to the waves of money circulating around the global marketplace—though almost certainly the movements that matter more are those we mentioned above by worried treasurers in search of currency safe havens and the best interest rates.

But the anti-globalizers protest that those decisions as well as the others, affecting thousands of employees, are taken outside their reach by people in other countries and cultures. That is where local directors have a role.

When Britain's new monetarist doctrine raised sterling's exchange rate from 3 deutsche marks to 5 deutsche marks, I was a local director of Goodyear Tire's subsidiary in the United Kingdom. The soaring pound turned steady profits into deep losses. I flew to Goodyear's world headquarters in Akron to see what I could do to avoid an immediate closure and the loss of the city of Wolverhampton's largest employer. I argued that that level of exchange was unsustainable, and that it would soon fall back (which it did). But I think that the plant was not saved by my argument or eloquence; it happened that both the international director and the board chairman had, in their time, managed the Wolverhampton plant and knew the people there.

But miracles like that are rare. A large U.S. electronics multinational was the biggest employer in a town in my electoral district. It had a well-organized public relations department who took me around this hive of purposeful activity, and I was most impressed. A couple of years later, it just pulled out; the hive of activity reduced to zero.

One reason why the presence of multinationals adds to the movement against such "globalization" is that they are not subject to the ordinary social contracts and disciplines of the society in which they work. Their brisk rotation of expatriate management does not make the job any easier. One local chairman of Goodyear asked me why the workforce didn't trust him. I said that he had been the third chairman in six years; they hadn't known him long enough. An American automobile company in Britain had a chairman who took great care of labor relations, which as a result were the best in the industry. His successor believed that "management should manage" and took only a year to wreck all that goodwill.

The continental European answer to such problems is legislation to protect the workers, who, if we compare the wages with the dividends, have a stake in the company several times greater than that of the shareholders—and their stake is a hundred percent of their income, compared with the fraction represented by the stake of an individual shareholder. It is far harder to dismiss workers in France or Germany than in the United Kingdom or United States, and far more notice has to be given of changes that will affect workers. In Germany the workers are represented, with the main shareholders, on an upper-tier board and are kept abreast of the company's activities. The Anglo-Saxon argument against such practices is that this removes the flexibility of management and makes the companies less competitive in international markets. But a comparison of the trading surpluses of the Euro-zone with the huge foreign trade deficits of Britain and the United States shows that that is not the way it has worked out.

GLOBAL MARKETS NEED NEW RULES

The postwar global institutions are now fifty years old, and the world has changed. The old institutions can no longer bear the weight put on them. The Bretton Woods Agreement, hammered out mainly between the United States and the United Kingdom in 1944, served well, but conditions have changed dramatically. The new creditor currencies are now those of the Euro-zone and the Japanese. The Cold War is now over, leaving a former super-power financially bankrupt and in need of far more than the grudging help given so far to make it a profitable and trustworthy trading partner. The Asian crisis brought the world money system close to meltdown. The time has come for stronger institutional safeguards.

Global money markets can be tamed only by agreement between the three main players—the United States, the Euro-zone, and the Japanese. Those nations alone have the weight of financial resources to make such a settlement stick. Reading the arguments leading to the postwar Bretton Woods Agreement, we can see that, even between the world's only two free countries, it was tough. Today, even though we have more experience, it would be even tougher. But free markets must have a stable monetary system, and there are some practical steps that the West could take.

For instance, there is no reason in international law why banks in any of these countries should be allowed to deal with tax havens. A firm stand on this issue would also cut off the traffic in dirty money from both drug barons and mafia. There should not be a majority in any democratic country, including Switzerland, that would want to maintain the privileges of tax havens.

The economic agenda of the West is regularly discussed by the

Group of Seven (the United States, Canada, Germany, the United Kingdom, France, Italy, and Japan, plus the representative of the remaining members of the European Union). It would be possible for the European Union, the United States, Canada, and Japan to agree to prosecute their own nationals for giving or taking illegal payments in another country. The process could be handled by an international court such as the ones that prosecute for crimes against humanity. The crime of bribery may not look so serious, but it is at the root of much civil strife, and action against it is a protection for the powerless and the innocent. The threat of indictment would almost certainly be decisive in drying up the sources of graft. Exporters and international contractors would be reassured that all their competitors would be subject to the same law, and everyone would know that a conviction would end their professional career.

The G-7 could also consider the regulation of the financial exposure of banks to overseas loans. Until now, the received wisdom has been that governments do not interfere with banks' lending decisions, and if the banks lose their loans in a crash, that's just tough. Since the Asian crisis of 1997, that policy is open to question. The swift recall of Western loans spread the crisis and could have turned the crash into a full-scale depression. So the unfettered action of the banks was not just a business decision. It created severe political risks. And the bailout of the Long-Term investment fund shows that, in the end, governments have to step in anyhow. Banking is a highly competitive business, and it is hard for a single bank to pass up business unless the same rules apply all around. So, after discussion with their overseas banks, the G-7 should set acceptable guidelines to establish boundaries on the exposure of banks to short-term overseas loans. The ultimate sanction would be no bailout for those who broke the guidelines.

Since the G-7 countries are the main paymasters for the IMF

and the World Bank, they should review the functions of those organizations. When the IMF and the World Bank were set up at the Bretton Woods conference, the Soviet Union was represented, but not Germany, Japan, or many of today's other major trading nations. Major European countries were only represented by governments in exile. Nearly sixty years later, the scale of international finance is vastly greater, and so are the problems. No one at Bretton Woods knew how the twin institutions to which they gave birth would stand up to the job. A review at this time would have sixty years' experience to draw on.

There is little doubt that any such review would advise much more flexibility, and also that there should be more liaison between the two institutions. A review might also conclude that both need more funds.

My own closest encounter with the IMF and World Bank was in 1992–1993, when, after the breakup of the Soviet Union, I wrote the European Parliament's reports on aid to Eastern Europe. As sadly reported in the previous chapter, the breakup of a superpower, with lethal nuclear capacity, produced the same standard package from the IMF as they would apply to any South American republic that had run out of credit—$1.5 billion unconditionally, or $5 billion on condition that they brought inflation under control.

The gut feeling of the protestors at and since Seattle is that something is wrong with our materialistic money-making system— that other values are left out of account. About that, every Christian should agree, they are right. But as we have tried to show, there are better ways of changing the world than their protests suggest.

8

The Electronic Economy

A while ago there was a very rich governor of British Columbia who had made his money by getting up early in the morning to call the London Stock Market and then Wall Street, so that by the time the Vancouver market opened he knew the trends and was well ahead of the game. Today the game never stops. The global economy would not be possible without the electronic economy. Its capacity to keep currency and stock markets in instant communication around the world may make banks and brokers more efficient, but it has also created a much more volatile market. There is no time to stop and think, only time to act; to get in before the market soars up again, or to get out that split second ahead of disaster.

The new technology not only makes communication faster, it also makes it much cheaper. So it is possible to have conference calls with participants from different countries, all of whom have the most up-to-date documentation in front of them. A conference call is more bland than face-to-face interaction, but it can get the bulk of the business done. And it can tighten control from the center. The global economy would be very different without the electronic economy.

If the electronic economy was there all along, as the global economy developed, what was new in the high-tech boom at the turn of the millennium? And why did the shares of high-tech companies collapse so fast?

THE ELECTRONIC ECONOMY IS NOT MAGIC

The high-tech boom of the 1990s seems to have been concentrated on the use of the Internet to replace retail shops and other labor-intensive personal services. The new "dot.com" stocks were heavily promoted, and the hope of investors was that "online" commerce would claim an ever-increasing percentage of retail business. So a lot of money went into a relatively limited share market and sent the prices rocketing up. As with all such booms, the price rise attracted other buyers, and the founders became paper millionaires. When the stock market turned down, these overvalued dot.com stocks fell fastest and farthest. Some of the inexperienced paper millionaires, in their anxiety to get ahead of the pack, spent more than their companies could afford on promotion, and some seem to have been plain extravagant. But there was and is nothing wrong with the major advance in technology.

The directors of one dot.com, all in their twenties, sat around the scrubbed wooden table on the stone flags of our old kitchen for their first board meeting. I told them to be clear about what business they were in and to stick to it. They decided that it was their business to give buyers a much wider choice than they could have in a shop or a printed catalog. Just as important, they agreed that it was not their job to warehouse, pack, or deliver goods, or to accept returns. And they had decided not to go to the public for finance. A year later, after the crash of the high-tech stocks, they were still there, one working full-time from his apartment and seven working part-time until their priced catalog and delivery arrangements were all set up.

Dot.com is not magic. It uses new technology to fill a gap in the market—in the case of these young entrepreneurs the decline in the big department store, which had offered a variety not available in today's specialist shops. And it helps those who do not have the time and energy to shop around, especially, perhaps, professional women.

THE GAINERS

The essential gain we have from the computer is its technical ability to make complex and interactive calculations at lightning speed. The effort to do this started with mechanically operated machines, the calculators in accountants' offices, the punch card machine, which did slowly and simply what computers now do a thousand times faster. I once used punch cards to set up a reordering system for a grocery chain buyer to tell him how each line was going, what his minimum stock should be, and when to reorder. Today the big trucks load up every evening with whatever the computer tells them to load, and travel through the night to keep the supermarkets' stocks at just the right level.

But the computer does not just do old tasks faster; it has the ability for interactive calculation with instant feedback—until now the preserve of humans, birds, fish, and animals. The computer is now interactive in the process of production, so that it can roll metal with greater precision than a human. It is interactive in the piloting of an aircraft, and can be even steadier than a pilot. And it can interact with sensors on the ground to bring the aircraft down to a blind landing that a pilot would never risk. It can take over production lines, chemical processes, and metal machining, and give a far higher degree of accuracy. It has removed a great swath of semi-skilled labor and has increased the demand for a smaller number of jobs with much higher skills.

In the newspaper industry, the computer has removed completely the need for the skilled printer in hot metal, and the journalist now types the final copy straight onto the template. The hospital scanner can pinpoint problems that could never be seen before. A handheld instrument can spot a deep-vein thrombosis. The computer is also a great help in scientific research, producing new drugs faster and also making diagnosis more reliable. When this computer technology is combined with the switch from copper to silicon cables, it is now possible to send far greater information along a single line, making all kinds of communication much cheaper and far faster. So we have an invention that is not just an incremental advance but a revolutionary change in the structure of our industrial society.

In my electoral district, Cambridge University encouraged the interchange of new ideas between its electronic engineers and industry. So salesmen and scientists met together in local pubs to look for development opportunities and then to persuade customers to finance the next generation. Trinity College opened a Science Park, and soon it became the center of high-tech industry, with new companies opening every month. The second oil shock brought high unemployment all over Britain, but in our corner, employment went up and up. There was the same pace of expansion in Silicon Valley in California and around Boston.

Around Cambridge, almost half of the high-tech companies were in medicine. It was not just the scanners; the new power of computation helps medical research find new drugs and new treatments far faster.

The electronic economy has rescued us from the tyranny of the production line. I remember standing by an old automobile production line. The activity of the men on the line was completely repetitive. They were nothing more than part of the machinery, doing the same boring job until the end of the shift. The production line treated human beings as if they were no more than a fractional horsepower engine with a cheap control mechanism.

The inflexibility made it hard to change the product, once the expensive production line had been set up. Alfred Sloan's annual model change at GM was an advance on Henry Ford's rule, "They can have any color they like so long as it's black." But underneath the flashy new tail fins, nothing much else changed. It was the computer that began to give back to industry its flexibility. When I was a CEO in the aluminum industry, the cost of a long standard production run was way below the cost of "specials," made as they were ordered. The new computer could run our whole order book through each morning to find that day's optimum production run on "specials," and that slashed their cost.

That was just a crude beginning. Today, not only production runs but the whole production process is governed by the computer. At the heart of the engineering industry is the machine tool, which used to depend on the skill of the operator. Today it is the computer that tells the machine how to carve out the exact and intricate patterns in metal. The processing industry, from sugar refining to chemicals, is also run by computer. Indeed it is hard to think of a major industry in which the precision, speed, and flexibility of the computer has not replaced manual skill. The development of the microchip was another great step forward, so that not only blind landing of aircraft but the performance of automobiles could be regulated.

The computer has brought back again business on a human scale. It is good that eight young people in their twenties can start up a dot.com company. As I visited the many high-tech companies in my electoral district, I was impressed by their enthusiasm. Even if I ran late on a tour and did not arrive until seven or eight in the evening, they were still there, glued to their computer screens. Some of those companies failed, but most of them seemed to succeed. There are no "passengers" in that size of company. I remember one company, making surgical instruments. It was tucked away in a business park behind a village main street. There was no receptionist. On the right of the tiny entrance was an office where one partner was talking to a customer in Chicago; and there was more noise behind the door on the left, where the other partner was looking after production.

All of us feel the personal benefits of new technology, especially in the far cheaper and faster communication given by the silicon cables. The lower cost and higher quality bring us as close to our American grandchildren as to those in London. The mobile phone doesn't even need cables. I always insist that my wife take hers when she drives out alone. A mobile phone helped a lost granddaughter find her way home. Even adults get lost and need to be guided to their destination.

GAINERS AND LOSERS IN MEDICINE

Medicine has been one of the great gainers from technology. Today an electronic scanner can locate cancers before they develop to lethal proportions and electronics can keep the surgeon on track during complex surgeries that would have been impossible before electronics came to the rescue. But these advances are expensive. My electoral district has one of our nation's best heart-transplant hospitals. It is not just a question of surgery. It needs foolproof equipment. Talking about the gory details of surgery is bad enough, but I have never seen anything like the flow of blood— the real blood of a living person under the surgeon's knife—going through all those glass tubes. Hospitals can't skimp on the hardware needed for heart transplants. But I recovered as soon as I saw the cheerful faces of the patients in the convalescent wards, for whom a new life lay ahead. A society based on a Christian moral order should want the same help for all.

Scanners are expensive. New and effective drugs can be expensive. My wife and I had the new antimalaria drug before going to lecture in Kenya. It is far more effective and had no side effects, but it is more expensive. So public health is faced with more costs; and with better health and a lot more elderly people, society is faced, at the same time, with the higher cost of pensions.

So these advances raise the issue of how much money the young and fit are prepared to give to the old and sick. We live with a cult of youth. High-tech industry itself is powered by the young. Our sports heroes are young and fit, and so are the television and film stars. We think of the old as boring, living in a past age, and with nothing more to contribute. We toy with the idea of euthanasia.

But we forget what we owe them. Two miles outside Cambridge is the American Military Cemetery at Madingley—row on neat row of gravestones. These were the young men who flew over Germany and didn't survive their last flight. We owe them for our victory over the tyranny that gassed six million Jews. But how about those who did survive, living among us in their 70s and 80s? Don't we owe them too? And there are those who fought later to save South Korea and Japan from communism. The names of the dead from Vietnam are all on that long wall in Washington. But most of those who survived are still with us.

It is not just the veterans we ought to respect. The generations before us built the prosperity that we now enjoy. It is easier for us, but it was tough for some of them. We owe them respect for what they have left us. We do not have to go so far in this as the Eastern religions that worship their ancestors. We have our heritage from the Jewish Scriptures, where the young, like David, listened to the old, like Samuel, and respected them. But those of us who are

Christians should be in no doubt: Christ gave priority to the healing of the sick, and so should we.

The issue is how much money the rich are prepared to give to looking after the old, the poor, and the sick. We can, and do, obscure that simple issue with endless arguments. But at the finish we have to ask ourselves whether, in a rich country, the poor get the medical treatment they need.

We looked earlier at the concern of Christians about abortion. An added argument against abortion is its massive diversion of skilled and qualified doctors and nurses to surgery for people who are young, fit, and well, which surely must have a material effect on the health care available to the sick and old. A great deal of health care money also goes into those who abuse themselves with drugs, alcohol, and tobacco.

There is another new burden on the work of doctors and nurses. I asked a senior nurse why they had to spend so much time on paperwork, so that most of the care had to be done by overworked juniors; what exactly had changed? The answer was that patients who did not get well were now liable to sue; the extra paperwork was protective. Every treatment has to be justified and every little thing has to be on the record. That could not be left to juniors. In America, the rush to litigation is probably even worse than it is in Britain. The problem is that a society that no longer believes in right and wrong is suspicious. At one time it was enough that moral standards were not only recognized but also rigidly enforced by professional bodies. If we could move back in that direction, there would be a lot more time for the patient, and much less pressure on medical resources.

As improved diagnosis and new drugs keep people alive longer, the biggest threat to medical ethics is the steadily mounting pressure for euthanasia. It is put in permissive terms: "Why keep the old alive when they want to die?" For the Christian the answer is simple: We are not allowed to take life, even if it is the life of the person who asks us to do so. And euthanasia would be dangerous for the medical profession, whose ethic is to preserve life. That is what gives them the trust they still enjoy. How could that trust be maintained as they used their skill to take life away? And if euthanasia were allowed, who would protect the old from greedy relatives who want to be rid of the cost of keeping them alive, and to get their hands on whatever property and money they will leave? Who could be sure that no pressure was put on an old woman, or that she was quite sure that she was signing her life away? It is the sin of a materialistic world to want to put elderly people on the trash heap when they cost more money than they bring in.

THE LOSS OF JOBS IN THE BIG CORPORATIONS

Electronics has taken over most of the work of the country's huge army of clerks. The airline ticket goes into a slot and you are checked through to board. Electronics can do more and more complex checks more reliably than any human check.

Ten thousand can lose their jobs in the downsizing of one big corporation. Maybe there will be jobs in the specialist phone centers, which now deal with the paperwork, or in the specialist call centers, which take orders. But maybe not. A big Welsh steel mill had just shut down and a man of about thirty said, over his garden gate, "I thought I had a job for life." There are no steel mills who want his specialist expertise, and there are thousands like him to swamp the local labor market.

Downsizing arrived in America during a decade of growth, at the end of which overall unemployment was only 4 percent, probably including people changing jobs. But with the end of the ten-year boom, the next decade may not be so easy. Structural change, with slower growth, is a major reason for higher unemployment in the European Union.

THE VULNERABILITY OF HIGH TECHNOLOGY

Another cost of change is the greater vulnerability of the high-tech structure. In the pen-pushing days, no one person could bring the whole of the stock exchange or all the currency markets to a halt. There were no hackers who could insert a virus to pervert every transaction. The world was not short of people with a grudge against society, but they had no access to the system. Today a hacker, working in a lonely room in Manila, can infect the American system coast to coast—and the rest of the world too! Just as a jet aircraft can be hijacked by one man with a gun, so one hacker can hijack a network serving millions.

It might not be so dangerous if we lived in an age when moral standards were still absolute and self-sustaining. But our age has decided that there is no absolute right and wrong; no religious leaders have the right to tell others how to live. So, as people take the law into their own hands and justify themselves by their own moral code, we live in an increasingly lawless society. The rich try to protect themselves by living in gated compounds. But the bars guarding our vital means of communication are still weak and vulnerable to losers who want to exercise power over the winners.

Even such simple a technology as the cell phone can disrupt the lives of those who had thought they were secure. In the millennium year, the main gas refineries of Britain were blocked by an alliance of farmers and small-time truckers, who demanded that government lower the tax on gas. The key to the organization of this disparate group was the mobile phone, so government could not cut their communications. The tanker drivers were unwilling to break the cordons outside the refineries, the oil companies did not want to order them to drive big, fully loaded tankers into a hostile crowd, and the police did not want to baton-charge a crowd of normally law-abiding citizens. The army did not have the tanker capacity to replace those in the refineries, and the government did not want to encourage mob rule.

Soon the gas stations began to run out of gas. The gas tanks in the supermarket depots also began to run out, and as the "just-in-time" deliveries failed, the supermarket shelves became bare. Only the airports had enough strategic reserves of fuel.

The strike failed because the truck owners and farmers came from the middle classes, who did not want to wreck the country. So friends and neighbors told the strikers to call it off, and government produced a face-saving formula. What the strike showed was that the mobile phone was a potent weapon in organizing action against the economic system. It also showed that, though it made sense for supermarkets to keep their stocks to the very minimum, "just-in-time deliveries" left the country highly vulnerable to disruption. But next time the threat could come from those who don't care what they do to friends and neighbors—if they have any.

THE GOOD AND THE BAD OF THE INTERNET

The Internet is an excellent means of communication. It makes whole libraries of information available. People who would not bother to go out to post a letter find themselves in touch by E-mail. We can download our favorite films, look at catalogs, and order clothes without going near a shop.

Like many men, I find shopping a bore and only do it when I must. But maybe the Net removes too much human contact. We have to be sure that the Net does not banish us from human company. What is true of adults is even more true of children, who can spend hours hunched over the screen in fantasy games when it would be a lot healthier for them if they were with their friends.

The other moral hazard of the Net is that it tempts us to do in private what, even in today's permissive society, we would not dream of doing in public. People who would not want to be seen buying a pornographic magazine can, with a few clicks, have "live" pornography on the screen. Western society has long since abandoned official censorship, but there are still social restraints. Pornography demeans women, making them into objects of lust, and most men do not want to be caught with overtly pornographic material. The secrecy of the Web removes this restraint. More important, it can make the worst kind of pornography open to children, although most parents will make sure that it is specifically programmed out.

However free we want our society to be, we still want to protect our children from abuse by pedophiles. But the Net is open to any group who wants to encourage each other, even if it is to this kind of antisocial action. The Net crosses national borders, so no national law can yet regulate what it carries. Despite these hazards, the Net keeps open the marketplace of ideas. So, for Christians, faced with press, television, and radio that are closed to anything but the secular mind-set, the Net spells freedom.

THE WIDENING GULF BETWEEN HIGH-TECH COUNTRIES AND THE REST OF THE WORLD

Until now, technological advance has closed down labor-intensive industry in the West and transferred it to countries where labor was much cheaper. Textiles led the way. The making of a traditional Eastern carpet is very labor-intensive. But the skill of a low-paid textile worker can almost certainly be replaced by the skill of a computer, and the actual machinery is common to both the high- and low-cost labor countries.

Even if that particular equation does not always come out to the advantage of the West, the West, by contrast with the rest of the world, is a knowledge economy. This superiority in scientific and technological knowledge does not at present enable the West to compete with the rest of the world in labor-intensive products. But that will no longer be true if computer-aided design and production can replicate the manual labor at lower cost. Poorer countries are doing their best to produce their own technical expertise. But even if they catch up, they are always at risk of losing their best brains to countries that can pay them five or ten times as much. The heads of the Russian defense industry saw the probable loss of their best brains to the West as their most vulnerable point. The main reason they would have accepted a "Marshall Plan" was that it would have enabled them to keep their scientists and engineers.

More Intensive Patterns of Work

There is little doubt that the pace of work is quickening. Businesses used to have middle ranks where there was a great deal of routine work, which once you were used to it did not take much emotional energy—today's move of the IN file to the OUT file was much the same routine as yesterday's. Downsizing has removed that whole pattern of life. Mechanical office work is now done by a machine. The remaining jobs need a good deal of hard thought, and that is a lot more tiring. And since the work is not to a pattern, it is easier to make mistakes, and that worry also saps our energy.

Previously, a lot of the job of the sales representative was routine reordering. Now the computer can calculate, from stock levels and sales levels, the timing and level of reordering. The sales representative has to concentrate on the tougher job or persuading a buyer to try a new line. Computer-aided design has taken a lot of the routine out of the design department. The designers now have to concentrate on the tougher job of making sure that the balance of the design fits as exactly as possible the balance needed in the product.

A generation or so ago, medical knowledge was simpler and

patients and their relatives did not have such high expectations. Now, as we have noted, far more can be done and far more is expected of doctors. Not only that, but if cures do not come up to expectations, doctors are liable to be sued. So they have to work harder and their anxiety level is higher. The pace and pressures of work are altogether different.

The pressure on managers is also much greater. The speed of communication makes for a more frenetic life. They can no longer leave their work behind at five o'clock. The mobile phone and the E-mail keep them in touch all the time. "Short-termism" has its own malign pressure. There is no time to wait until long-term plans pay off. If the next quarter's earnings per share are not up, then there may be a hostile bid for the company. That works down to the subsidiary companies in the group. If they do not produce the needed rise in profits, they may be sold off and gain a new and unknown set of bosses.

Maybe, especially at the top level and in business consultancy, the problem is the sheer power of number crunching. Before that formidable power was at hand, decisions had to be made from what rough numbers were available and on back-of-the-envelope calculations. This drew discussion on to the high points, which would swing the decision. It also gave as much weight to the credibility of the people on whose experienced business judgment the decision turned. The problem with figures, as all accountants used to learn, is that they look much more precise than they are. Every figure in a balance sheet or revenue account is based on assumptions. The job of the public accountant is to test those assumptions. The number crunchers should remember the saying, "Rubbish in, rubbish out."

Projections on mergers and acquisitions are the stuff of modern consultancy. Corporations and their consultants shuffle the deck to make sure of higher earnings per share for the next quarter, and the number cruncher pours out the figures. If these are not acceptable, then the junior-level consultants have to work through the night and maybe over the following weekend so that the board can look at a more acceptable combination. Maybe I exaggerate, but I doubt it.

MISSILE TECHNOLOGY

Until the end of the Cold War, the West was under the constant threat of a nuclear weapon strike. During the Cuban missile crisis the threat was very real. I was in New York at the time; there were only two other people in the vast auditorium of the largest cinema in Times Square. That excellent film, *Thirteen Days,* gives a day-by-day account of the crisis, based on the recently released White House tapes. I had known that it was a close call, but had never realized how close.

Since then there have been treaties between the Warsaw Pact nations and NATO to stop the nuclear race and guarantee "no first strike." There have also been treaties aimed to avoid proliferation of nuclear weapons by countries outside NATO and the Warsaw Pact. At the breakup of the Soviet Union, as we have seen, the West worried that the weapons might get into the wrong hands. But Russia has taken over the U.S.S.R. treaty obligations and continues mutual East/West policies to contain the spread of nuclear weapons.

The death in war of innocent civilians is inevitable; but, in revulsion against the mass bombings of World War II—both the nuclear bombings and the firestorms in Dresden and Hamburg—Western military strategy has since then aimed to destroy the armed forces of the enemy, not women and children. At a discussion between top military and civil servants and church leaders on the ethics of nuclear war, both church and military were agreed. The church opposed the use of nuclear weapons because they could not be deployed in such a way as to avoid the deaths of millions of civilians. The armed forces said that they would sooner spend the money on tanks, aircraft, or ships, and said that nuclear bombs were not weapons of war but instruments of mass slaughter.

Just before the breakup of the Soviet Union, a possible new technology appeared, the antimissile missile, at once christened "Star Wars" by its detractors. The European Parliament/U.S. Congress delegations met shortly afterwards. At a lunch at the Senate, Senator Lugar explained the administration's view and Senator Joseph Biden attacked it. Then we had a long discussion with our House colleagues, appropriately held at the United States Military Academy at West Point. We found the congressmen very skeptical. But one old Southern Democrat said that though he didn't believe in the feasibility of "Star Wars," he would vote for it because the Soviets would have to try to match it, and that would finally bankrupt them.

We moved on to the Pentagon, where a French colleague, Didier Motchane, summed up our other reason for skepticism: "There is a fatal flaw in your Star Wars, Mr. Weinberger. You cannot know whether it will work until you push the button; and by then, it is too late."

Within a few years, the Soviet Union collapsed, crushed by military expenditure; and for a long time, little was heard of "Star Wars." Now the idea is again in the news.

It is, of course, human nature to want to build walls to keep out hostile forces. The Great Wall of China, the walls of ancient Babylon, the castles that litter Europe, and France's 1939 Maginot Line were, in their time, the latest expensive technological solution to national defense. Fast German tanks outflanked the Maginot Line, gunpowder dealt with the castles, and the Medes diverted the River Euphrates and entered Babylon one night along the dry riverbed.

But there is another problem with building walls. It tempts our enemies to take action while there is time, before the wall is securely in place. It seemed, from our West Point discussions, that it would take a long time before a safe antimissile shield was in place. The long interval prior to its arrival would destabilize the careful balance of power, which had kept nuclear weapons out of use for half a century. Countries would have to consider the effect on the rest of the world if the largest nuclear power were able to put itself out of range of everyone else. The nuclear balance held for half a century because both sides were equally at risk. Now, even allies would have to consider the balance within the alliance if they were completely dependent on a shield that could be withdrawn at any time with no risk to the holder. Our feeling was that, whether or not it worked in the end, the long research and development of the missile shield brought far more problems than it would solve when, if ever, it was completed.

I do not see that anything has changed.

9

THE GOOD LEADER

"The buck stops here."
PRESIDENT HARRY S. TRUMAN

Christians are not pessimists. We analyze what has gone wrong in order to do our best to put it right. Christ has told us to be the salt in our society, preventing its total corruption. And we believe that, whatever he wants us to do, he will give us the gifts and strength to do it. There are Christians in all walks of life, but there is a special burden on those who have the gifts of leadership. So this last chapter will focus on the kind of leadership we need to turn our societies around.

Leaders are essential at all levels, from leaders of youth groups and captains of football teams right up to the five-star general and the president of the United States. Most of us will be leaders at some time or another. Even if we are quiet and unobtrusive—perhaps just because we are quiet—someday, someone, somewhere, will look to us for leadership.

The Bible gives us some vivid pictures of leaders, and it is a better guide than most because it shows all the faults of the leaders as well as their virtues. And it also shows that none of them set out to become leaders. But somewhere along the line, they had a vision of what they had to do and why.

THE LEADER'S VISION

Moses had a real vision in the desert of Sinai: a burning bush that did not burn up, an awesome voice that called on him to lead the children of Israel out of Egypt. He didn't want to do it. He had been a shepherd for forty years. He had a wife and family, and he did not want to go back to Egypt. When told to confront Pharaoh, Moses protested that not even his own people Israel would listen to him, let alone Pharaoh. He pleaded that his brother was the eloquent one of the family. Moses did go back to Egypt, to his people and to the court where he had been brought up. And with God's power, this reluctant man rose to the occasion, confronted the most powerful ruler in the world, and led his people for the next forty years.

David's vision was also slow in coming. He was the youngest son in a large family; when the prophet Samuel came to Bethlehem and asked to see all of Jesse's sons, it did not occur to Jesse to send for the young, music-loving shepherd boy, who was out with the flocks. It was as a musician that the king's advisers first suggested he send for David, and he was so unobtrusive that when the king next encountered him, he had to ask who he was.

That was when the compulsion to lead first came to David. Who was this huge Philistine who cursed the living God? Why was no one going out to fight him? So strong was David's outrage that he volunteered to do the job himself. The armor was too clumsy, but he could aim a stone from his sling at a hairsbreadth. And so, alone, he killed Goliath.

Soon David was a leader in the army, making raids on the Philistines; and soon, too, he was so successful that the people cheered him more than they cheered Saul. But David had no intention of building on his own popularity to overthrow the king, who was "God's anointed" and who would surely be succeeded by David's best friend, Jonathan.

When David was driven to the desert, heading a band of four

hundred other outlaws and hounded by Saul, he had Saul's life in his hands twice and still would not seize the throne. Only when Saul and Jonathan had both been killed in the disastrous battle on Mount Gilboa did David begin to see his inexorable destiny, that Samuel's anointing in front of his family all that time ago had been the call to be king. But even then, he waited for the elders of Judah to call him to the throne, and he waited another seven years for the summons from the northern tribes.

The vision of the high Pharisee on the road to Damascus was much more dramatic. He was told there and then what his future was to be. He did have a time of reflection and instruction, but the vision never changed—how could it? He was the Apostle to the Gentiles, the first to take the Christian faith to Europe and, finally, to the court of the emperor at the heart of Rome. Even in prison, Paul's vision never failed.

Fast-forward fifteen hundred years to a young monk studying the Bible and trying to reconcile it with the teaching of a corrupt church. The story is that, kneeling step by step up Rome's Santa Scala toward the altar at the top, he suddenly saw that the Bible and the church's teaching on salvation from sin could not be reconciled. One was right and the other was wrong. He stood up and walked down the stairs, clear that his duty was to teach what he had found in God's Word, whatever became of him. It was that vision, not his ambition, that propelled Martin Luther into leadership. It was that vision that made him say, in front of the Emperor, "Hier stehe ich; ich kann nicht anders" ("Here I stand, I can do no other").

Fast-forward another three hundred years, to a time when the vision of Martin Luther and the great Reformers had faded. Another group, as earnest as the young Luther, had a vision of a Christian life that was so disciplined that there could be nothing wrong or out of place. They had the nickname of "methodists." But however worthy, it was a low-level, mundane vision, a life of self-imposed rules and regulations. Then one day one of the group, John Wesley, was at a Moravian service in London, and he said of the experience, "I felt my heart strangely warmed."

It was this warm faith in the love of God, who sent his Son to die for our sins, that gripped Wesley. He, too, did not set out to be a leader, but as he went up and down the country preaching in the open air—because the churches would not give this young clergyman a pulpit—there were converts; and the converts formed groups, the groups found local leaders, and, though he would not admit it, John Wesley found himself, at the end of his long life, the founder and leader of a new church, which wore with pride its old nickname of "Methodist."

God does not give us gifts as the rich might throw money to the poor. He gives, as these five stories show, particular gifts to particular people, and included in that range of gifts is the gift of leadership. To some like Paul, who was already a leader, he shows at once how the gift of leadership is to be used. To others the gift comes more slowly, and they find themselves leaders despite themselves as they realize that others now depend on them to achieve their common vision.

DEFINING OUR OBJECTIVES

But even where we cannot claim divine vision, we should still have aims for whatever job we are given to do. An army unsure of where it is going is soon cut down. I used to work with a retired general and, whenever I discussed some project, he would ask precisely, "What is the object of the exercise?" At Staff College they taught future leaders that they must first work out clear objectives. Only then could they begin to plan how to achieve them.

Moses knew that his objective was to lead his people to the Promised Land. David knew that he should defend a united kingdom from its enemies. Paul's objective was to bring the Christian message to the Gentiles, Luther's to reform the faith, and Wesley's to preach the gospel and rebuild the church.

There was a single-mindedness about all of them, a refusal to be deflected from what they knew was their proper job. There must also have been, in each of them, a feeling that unless they gave a strong lead, the work would not be done; that hundreds of thousands of people depended on their leadership. But it was the vision of what could and must be achieved that kept them going when times got tough.

If we are a school principal, we must have a vision of the school we would like to see. A CEO must see what the enterprise could and should achieve. A pastor should want to see a well-taught church, showing Christian love to the people around them, especially those in need. Unless we have such a vision, we are driven along from crisis to crisis and never achieve anything.

THE WELL-EQUIPPED LEADER

Moses, who gave God's law to Israel and who acted as its judge for forty years, was not just a shepherd from the back side of the desert. Before his shepherding days, he had been brought up as a prince of Egypt at the court of Pharaoh. And Egypt was not just any old nation. It was the most powerful, most civilized country in the known world. As a prince, Moses would have had a thorough grounding in Egyptian law. He would also have had a knowledge of Egyptian dietary laws, sanitary laws, and medicine. Thus the law from Sinai was laid down by God but was passed on to the people by a man who knew something of the reason for those laws. The laws of Moses were a safeguard against infectious diseases three thousand years before modern science showed us precisely how infectious diseases were passed on—why, for instance, birds of prey and shellfish were dangerous to eat (Lev. 11:9-19). Had medieval Europe followed the laws of Moses, they would not have suffered the great plague!

By age forty Moses would have known how to weigh evidence, would have been able to sort out the liars from those telling the truth, and would have had the courage and self-confidence to sentence the guilty and release the innocent. It is clear from the advice given to him by his father-in-law, Jethro, that Moses thought he was the only person who had the competence to do all this (see Exodus 18).

Also, as a prince of the ruling family, Moses would have known how to deal promptly with rebellion and would have known the need to put it down before it spread.

But although he had been an adopted prince in Egypt, Moses had had his own mother as his nurse, so he would also have known all the teaching about God that had been passed down from the Patriarchs, Abraham, Isaac, and Jacob, and in his own tribe of Levi. So he knew a moral law very different from that of the Egyptians.

None of that preparation would have been any good had Moses not also have had a very different experience: how to survive in the desert of Sinai, where he had fled after killing an Egyptian for mistreating a fellow Israelite. There in the desert Moses met the daughter of Jethro, who kept large flocks, and he married her and looked after his father-in-law's flocks. He knew the desert tracks and, above all, where to find the water in that arid and hostile place to preserve the children of Israel and their flocks. Israel was led by a man who knew the ways of the desert, and how to keep out of range of hostile tribes.

David did not aim to be king, but God gave him the training. It was he and not King Saul who led the successful raids against the hostile Philistines; and, if that were not enough, he was forced to lead and lick into shape the four hundred outlaws who had gathered with him in the southern borders of Israel.

They moved together, evading Saul's clumsy pursuit, attacking the raiding bands from over the border, relieving the town of Keliah; and, now six hundred strong, they peeled off from the Philistine army and marched from Mount Moriah back to their base and, when they found that their camp had been raided and their wives and children taken, they marched straight on after the Amalekites and defeated them after a battle that lasted a whole day.

That was where David and his leaders learned the swift movement that enabled them to march from one end of the country to the other and pounce on unwary enemies. And it was where David's thirty "mighty men" learned their leadership too.

The apostle Paul's training was quite different. He was an outstanding academic in the school of Gamaliel; as he put it himself, he was "a Pharisee of the Pharisees." No one knew the prophetic Scriptures better than he did. Then, suddenly, his world was turned upside down, and he needed a time apart to put it together again. He did not go to the other apostles for instruction; he just needed time to search the Scriptures with his new insight into the true meaning of the Messianic prophecies.

It was this combination of Old Testament knowledge and Christian revelation that gave us the great doctrinal statements of the Pauline letters to the Romans, Galatians, Ephesians, Philippians, and Colossians, as well as his letters to Timothy and Titus. It must also have been a factor in convincing the other apostles in the Council at Jerusalem that the Gentile Christians did not have to keep to the ceremonial law of the Jews. Above all, the teachings of Paul's letters were the centerpiece of the great confessions of the Christian faith, which refuted the heresies that tried to water it down with Greek and other philosophies.

Luther was a monastic scholar before he was a leader of the Reformation, and it was his study of Paul's letter to the Romans that convinced him that the church's teaching no longer reflected the Christian message of God's free offer of forgiveness for those who trust in Christ's atoning death. Underlying Luther's courage was a powerful intellectual conviction based on his studies.

Wesley too was a scholar, and the "Methodist" movement started in the University of Oxford. He was persuaded in his mind before his heart was changed. And he, too, had the broad grounding in Christian theology needed for his preaching and teaching, which over the next fifty years created a new church, no longer dependent on the rule of worldly bishops.

For a lot of us the period of training is tough, and we may wonder whether we will ever use the knowledge and disciplines we achieved at such cost to our social life. I would never again want to go through the tedious grind of training to be an accountant. My history studies at the university had been full of life and color, but accounting was deadly and exacting detail. Both sides of the balance sheet must add up exactly. One dollar out and it was wrong. But it made the mind work overtime. You became a detective, asking whether the figures before you were valid or false. The break came on the day I worked out that the elaborate schedules I had been given proved the exact opposite to what they claimed. Years afterwards, my studies in accounting have left me with a useful knack of getting to the heart of a problem.

DELEGATION

The one skill many leaders find very difficult is delegation. They find it hard to believe that anyone else can do it as well as they can, and that it isn't faster to do it yourself than to explain it to others. Also, proper delegation needs to be thought through and organized, and there is always something more important to do. But our five great leaders all delegated.

Moses had to be persuaded to delegate. Jethro paid him a visit and sat in while Moses heard all the cases that came before him. Afterwards Jethro told him, as only he could, that Moses was wearing himself out and that he ought to delegate his duties to judges from each tribe and deal only with the hard cases himself. Being a wise man, Moses agreed, and from there on, that was how it was done.

As soon as he became king over Judah instead of a leader of six hundred outlaws, David delegated the army to Joab as commander in chief. As the kingdom developed, he had commanders of twelve divisions of 24,000 men, and under them commanders of thousands and of hundreds; there were officers over the tribes and overseers over all the civil works. He also had an inner cabinet of three or four special advisers.

But delegation does not mean that you opt out completely. The soldiers want to see their king. After the defeat of the Ammonites, Joab besieged their capital but David stayed behind in Jerusalem and, in an idle moment, committed adultery with the wife of one of his thirty trusty leaders, a close companion from the days when they were outlaws together. Worse, he asked Joab to put his faithful friend in the front line, where he was killed. Though he repented and recovered, David lost the respect a leader needs, and not much went right for him from then on.

Paul's method of delegation was to appoint leaders in all the churches he had founded, to visit them again whenever he could, and to write to them when he couldn't visit. Then he delegated the work to people like Timothy and Titus and, when he was imprisoned, the delegation became complete and everyone had to learn how to stand on their own feet.

When Luther's home state of Saxony had broken with Rome, Luther saw the pressing need to make sure that the Saxon churches were capable of teaching the people. He visited the churches and also helped them develop forms of service and hymns that reflected the Reformed doctrine. The structure of the Lutheran church is a monument to his delegation of the Reformation to the parish level.

Wesley had a tougher job. The Methodist societies were not originally meant to be churches. But in the absence of a state church to give the new converts the teaching they needed, the societies took over and, though John Wesley remained an ordained Episcopal clergyman to the end of his days, he spent his time going from society to society to see that they had the leadership and teaching that their people needed, and that they looked after the poor and anyone else who could not look after themselves.

PATIENCE AND PERSEVERANCE

Moses kept on asking Israel how long he should put up with them. Once they were rescued from the Egyptians and were safely across the Red Sea, they started to grumble. When Moses came down from Sinai, he found them worshiping a golden calf. Then there was Korah's rebellion. When the spies came back from the Promised Land, the very people God had rescued from the mighty Egyptian army quaked at the thought of the tribes of Canaan. But Moses' patience held firm. He did the job God had given him for forty more years, until a new generation was prepared to take the land God had promised them.

We find David endlessly patient with King Saul. Even when Saul throws a spear at him, he comes back again. He only leaves the court when Jonathan warns him to stay away. As an outlaw, he refuses to do anything against the king whom the Lord has anointed, even though Saul's life is twice in his hands. When at last David is king of Judah, he waits seven years for the northern tribes to ask him to be king. He will not take the kingdom by force.

Paul, too, we find endlessly patient with the Jewish synagogues that, in town after town, will not listen to this eminent Pharisee who teaches that Jesus is indeed the Christ. Paul leaves a town only when forced to leave. His patience in his years of imprisonment comes through clearly in his letters. It is in God's hands; he is "a prisoner of Jesus Christ" (e.g., Philem. 1). Not many of us have that kind of patience. And in the letter to Philemon, though Paul does not overtly instruct that slave-owner to set free the newly converted runaway slave, Onesimus, his appeal to him in the gentlest and most irresistible language leaves Philemon no alternative.

After his confrontation with the Catholic Church and the emperor, Luther was taken to the security of a great castle. There he patiently spent his time in studying and writing. He was in God's hands, and would wait on God's time.

John Wesley was excluded from the pulpits of his own church, so he took to preaching in the open air instead, and he and George Whitefield reached far more people in the open air than they would ever have reached in a church.

The other side of patience is perseverance. If we cannot do it now, then we are prepared to wait. Leaders today are expected to be men and women of action, who have a positive agenda, who sweep barriers to one side to get on with it. Though that is the image on film and television, a real leader is more realistic. No one can lead a team of professionals without patience, and certainly no one with a quick temper can head an organization employing thousands of people.

Patience is not the same as lethargy. Patience is waiting until the key problems have been solved, until everyone is on board, until opposition has died down. Big projects in big organizations need broad support, and that takes time.

John Hume did not win the Nobel Peace Prize by taking shortcuts in trying to settle the divisions between Unionist and Nationalist in Northern Ireland. He had the patience for lengthy discussions with Sinn Fein leaders at a time when no one else in Britain or Ireland would talk to them. And slowly he persuaded them that they would never reach their goal by force, but that they could gain most of what they wanted through the political process. Then he had the job of persuading the British and Irish governments that Sinn Fein was in earnest, and then to get them to lay down the ground rules for a new beginning. After the two governments' joint declaration, there had to be a referendum and then the long, exasperating, difficult negotiation before there was a new constitution, elections, and a new Northern Ireland Assembly, where Sinn Fein, Hume's own party (the SDLP), and the Unionists sat down together and elected an administration to represent them all. The quietly spoken French teacher, drawn into politics to protect his neighbors, was a true leader.

There's no doubt that some situations need "action today." And that's fine. But a leader who tries to put all problems on the fast track will soon crash.

Patience is not a passive quality. With patience goes persistence. We have to go on working on the problem, trying every angle, bringing everyone on board. It's the difference between democracy and dictatorship. Democracy brings lasting solutions; dictatorship only stores up resentment and trouble for the future. There are no shortcuts.

And we Christians have to remember that we believe in a patient God, who is prepared to wait because he wants "all people everywhere" to repent and be saved (Acts 17:30).

COURAGE

Finally, leadership requires courage. Moses did not want to go back to Egypt, because he knew the weight of the commission God had asked him to accept. He prevaricated, saying that he was not sufficiently eloquent. He knew perfectly well that no amount of eloquence would move the most powerful leader in the world; but God answered him on his own terms and told him to take his brother Aaron with him as a spokesman. And God gave Moses himself all the eloquence he needed, face-to-face with the man who could order his instant execution as a troublemaker. God was on Moses' side, and, finally, it was the frightened Egyptians who insisted that the Israelites get out of their country as quickly as possible and who gave them all they needed for the journey.

That was not the end of Israel's troubles. They were pinned between Pharaoh's army and the sea, and Moses held them steady. When Moses was on Mount Sinai, the people insisted on making an idol, and Aaron did not stand up to them; Moses had to take on everyone in sight, but he did. Then there was Korah's rebellion, and again Moses stood up to the rebels; and for a long forty years his courage kept them going until, at last, there was a new generation prepared to take the people over the Jordan.

Of David's courage there can be no question. From the single-handed attack on Goliath, to his leadership of Saul's army, to his courage as leader of an outlaw band and his victories, first against the Philistines and then against all of Israel's powerful neighbors, David led from the front. Except for that one fatal occasion when he stayed in Jerusalem, he went on leading until his strength finally gave out and his guard had to come to his rescue (2 Sam. 21:17).

Paul's courage knew no bounds. When he was finally convinced of the Christian faith, this former Pharisee leader went straight to the opponents of the faith and told them why he was a Christian. He was set upon by hostile mobs, stoned, imprisoned, flogged, shipwrecked, hungry and thirsty, and abandoned by those who should have stood by him. But none of these disasters could stop Paul from spreading the Christian message. He went back to Jerusalem, the heart of the opposition, against all warnings.

Luther defied the emperor, the most powerful ruler of his day, knowing that he also had the power of the Roman church against him. He did not have to go to the emperor to argue his case. He could have stayed within the protection of his own friendly state of Saxony. He knew that he had outraged the powerful leaders of both empire and church. But he felt compelled to argue the case for the Reformation, risking life and liberty. He could not foresee, when he went into the lion's den, that he would escape as he did from the surrounding troops, and would be safely hidden from the wide searches of all who wanted his life. It was on Luther's courage that the Reformation depended.

John Wesley and the other Methodist leaders preached in the open air, away from all the restraint and good manners of church congregations, where the poor, if they attended church at all, were kept in their place. If a mob gathered in the open, there was no one to keep them in order. If stones were thrown, there was no defense. If the speaker was surrounded, there was no easy escape. It was out there in the open that the roughest class of society—like the miners of Bristol—came in their thousands and were gripped by the message and converted. But John Wesley and Charles Wesley and George Whitefield did not know of that wonderful outcome when they first faced the crowds.

Not only that, but they risked the wild and hazardous north Atlantic gales in small sailing ships as they crossed and recrossed the Atlantic to bring their message to the States, from Georgia to New England.

There are Christians in our day who still have to have that kind of physical courage. The Chinese church suffered much under the rule of Chairman Mao—and grew at a record rate.

But though there is formal freedom of religion in most countries at the beginning of the twenty-first century, the climate is implacably hostile to those whose faith is more than mere membership in the social club that we call the church. The climate of moral permissiveness and blind materialism permeates most of the institutions in which we earn our living, and there may come a time when we are pressed to keep in line. Then, whatever the cost, we will have to step down rather than accept responsibility for policies we believe to be morally wrong.

How Do Others See Their Boss?

When you ask people what is the main problem in their job, they say, as often as not, that it is their boss. Maybe they should think through what it is that their boss needs from them. But those who are bosses should take note that people who work for them may see them as their major problem.

Bosses come at all levels, from the directors of a great multinational in the Fortune 500 to the owner of a garage with three employees. Most of us are, or one day will be, somebody's boss, somewhere up or down a line of management in a hospital, police force, sales team, school, church, or industrial plant. We know that what we do and how we do it matters to those above us, because they hold our paycheck and our future in their hands. But the way we behave also matters to those below us. We can help or hinder them in their job; we can either make them feel encouraged and empowered or keep them awake nights with worry.

I have visited more schools and plants than most people. In one year I walked around fifty plants, large and small. In all these plants it was possible to tell, almost at once, whether personal relations were good or bad. Where they were bad, the management talked about the machinery and ignored the people. In those with good relations, the people were introduced by name, with some account of what they were doing—and even of their hobbies— "Jim is a champion angler; he fishes with shore lines."

I visited one plant with a warmhearted, friendly member of the government who insisted on talking to everyone, while perspiration rolled down the face of the plant manager, who knew none of them. At the next plant, the boss introduced everyone, even the apprentices, with great pride. I was not surprised when the first plant had a prolonged and bitter strike not long afterwards.

Of course it is not just a matter of glad-handing and memorizing names and hobbies. It is trying, in all we say to them, to see the job from their point of view. We do it with customers; we should do it with those we employ as well.

The best boss I ever had taught me the courtesies of great men. "If you are not going to appoint an applicant for a job," he said, "tell him at once, because he will be applying for other jobs too and will need to know." If you wrote an opinionated letter, he simply ignored it, leaving it to you to think it over and decide that you had been foolish. (I never sent him that kind of letter again!) He saw everyone who reported to him at least once a month and listened, unhurried, while they talked. If you did something outstanding, he would be the first to praise you. If he supported you in a hard decision, he would never let you down, even when the going got really rough. His was no easy courtesy. He was as tough as they come, and he saw the weak point in any proposal with the speed of light, so it was worth going over it with a fine-tooth comb before you put it before him. He has been my role model ever since.

A FAIR WAGE

The apostle Paul tells us that wages should be "right and fair" (Col. 4:1). And we should try to treat everyone fairly too. It means equal treatment for equal work; but that is the easy part. Anyone who has ever tried to work out a "just wage" knows how hard it is to find the right yardsticks and the right differentials for skill and service. We have to take into account all the different kinds of skills, and calculate the amount of work, risk, responsibility, and hardship in each different kind of job. No one can get it exactly right, but at least we should try, comparing, for instance, with others in our trade or profession. No one expects perfection, but everyone expects an effort to get it as near as we can.

There are times when bargaining simply doesn't work and strikes go on forever. Flying from Melbourne to Sydney, I could see a fleet of ships lying off one of the east coast ports. The longshoremen had been on strike for months and I was glad we were not doing business there.

But trade union power does not seem to be the problem today. The U.S. level of union membership is not much more than a tenth of all employees. In Britain too, union membership has dropped. Employers have taken a lot of care in the last two decades to reduce their vulnerability to strikes. They spread their sourcing around so that no one supplier's strike can put them in trouble. Production lines are also scattered—including investment overseas—so that one line out of action cannot hold the company to ransom, and a good deal more work is subcontracted. The workforce knows too that their home market is vulnerable to competitive imports. So, one way or another, union bargaining power has evaporated.

That makes it all the more important for employers to be fair. It is best, if we can, to pay more than the national average. That attracts and keeps good workers and puts pressure on management to improve productivity and sales, to come up with new products and new ideas. Employers also need to be fair between workers, giving them the same rate for the same work and paying more for greater skills and responsibility. These are the practices of every good employer; but we need to be sure that they are the practices of churches and other voluntary bodies too.

Trade unions are not the only people who try to set wage levels. The older professions, which demand a high degree of skill because of their importance to society, ask their members to charge a minimum scale. Because of their importance to society, they need to encourage a steady supply of new entrants. Engineers or architects do not create a demand for their services by cutting their fees.

Management can divide surpluses three ways: to the employees, to the shareholder, and to the customer. Long term, companies can stay in business only if they give the customer competitive value, either by improving the product or service or by cutting costs to keep the price down. Short term, they have to pay competitive wages and maybe pay above the average to keep key workers and staff. The problem today is the much more powerful short-term pressure of the stock market, which we have discussed. Top management should try to keep a balance, but today it is tough at the top.

LIMITS OF MANAGEMENT AUTHORITY

Management cannot take responsibility for what their employees do outside the business. But if, for instance, the manager of a plant in a small town became a known drunkard or womanizer, then he probably would not have the local respect needed to do his job as an employer.

The toughest case I had was the allegation that a manager had got a young woman from another department drunk at an office party and had taken her back to his hotel room and sexually abused her. He said that he had taken her to his room because she was too drunk to go home. Her own boss believed the woman and said that, since it was an office party, we bore some responsibility. The man's boss backed him, and he was senior to the woman's boss. The company chairman said that it was not our responsibility to be moral judges of behavior outside the office. But the questions were whether an office party was "outside the office" and whether an office relationship had been abused. There were other ethical conflicts in the company at the time, and after a few anxious months I found another job.

Today we have a much more permissive climate of opinion outside the office; but with more women in jobs, young and attractive and working closely with men, laws against sexual harassment have been passed to protect them. So, where my chairman backed off, the law today would step in. But the law is a very blunt instrument, and those women who bring cases that are reported in the press may wonder whether they will ever get another job.

A good boss should be aware of all this and try to create conditions of work that minimize the risk of sexual harassment, and also to employ people who, as far as can be judged, can be trusted to work well in mixed company.

FIRING PEOPLE

The worst job is to tell someone that you no longer need them, and the worst of all is closing down a whole plant. There may be people who think no Christian should ever fire anyone, let alone fire a whole workforce. But the boss has to think of the whole team, and if some are not pulling their weight, they are a burden on everyone else and may put the whole group's work and reputation at risk.

The same goes for the closure of a loss-making plant. Such an operation is using up the dollars for the new products needed to keep the company's place in the market. No company can go on subsidizing unwanted products, thus risking the resources needed to make products customers do want.

I once had to close a specialized high-quality plant. The market had turned down, and we could get all the volume we needed from the bigger and lower-cost plants. We worked out a deal for the plant, offering transfer to everyone and generous compensation to those who did not accept the transfer. We consulted the trade union, who thought it a model deal. I saw the staff first and then the whole workforce, told them why we had to do it and what we were offering. The least you can do is to see them eyeball to eyeball. Less than ten percent took the transfer—family ties were too strong—and most of the rest found other jobs.

Firing individuals is tougher, especially ones you have taken on yourself. But if, for one reason or another, people don't fit in the team, it is better to encourage them to find some place where they do fit. I have, over time, made four high-level outside appointments when, had I had more patience, I would have promoted an insider. All those who left went on to jobs where they fitted better and did well. And the inside promotions made far better teams.

The toughest of all was when I took over the chair of a voluntary organization. The former director, whose vision and energy had built up the organization, had overspent the budget and had been sidelined. But he was a big man and needed a big job. I suggested to him that he find one, and then we could look for his successor. He had wide connections and in no time at all was running an extremely successful consultancy. Every time I met him, he told me how grateful he was to me for making him take the plunge.

But there are, and always will be, people who are just not up to the job. I insisted, against the finance director, on the early retirement of an elderly accountant. He came to see me afterwards to say how relieved he was. He knew he could no longer do the job, and it had made his life a misery. But maybe those two success stories are exceptions.

There are sales directors who lose market share and have to be replaced promptly if the company and all it employs is going to stay in business. There are plant managers whose incompetence risks the jobs of a thousand workers. If you are in the hot seat, you have to protect the majority against the individual who is not up to the job.

THE GREATEST LEADER

The greatest leader in history is Christ himself.

Jesus started with a team of twelve leaders. They were an unlikely group, some plain fishermen, one a tax collector, and one, though this did not appear until the last, a traitor.

They came with him as he taught the people and, incidentally, taught them too. Alone again, they asked questions on points they did not understand. Jesus taught them to care for people, to feed the hungry and not send them away. By healing, he taught them that God cares for our health as well. By his social habits, he taught them that God cares for every kind of person, whatever their background, but that if they have been sinners, he wants them to repent and change their ways. He warned them against the errors of the religious leaders of the day, and told them that governments, even alien governments, were there for a purpose and were entitled to ask for taxes. And he taught them not to be ambitious, for, in his kingdom, "the first will be last, and the last first" (Mark 10:31). In the toughest lesson of all, Jesus taught them that his was not the earthly kingdom that all Jews expected but a spiritual kingdom that would last forever.

In the middle of this, when he knew that they were ready, he sent them out on their own. If people did not want to listen, they were to pass on, but they were to stay and teach those who would listen.

Finally, after three years, Jesus left them to pass on his teaching and to establish his spiritual kingdom, which is the leading religion in the world today.

CHRISTIAN LEADERS

Church leaders need our special support, because they are especially vulnerable. One of the twelve apostles betrayed Jesus and another denied that he even knew him. There is always pressure on those at the forefront of the spiritual battle for souls and minds.

The church is the throbbing heart of Christ's kingdom and, of the "viruses" that attack it, those aimed at the leadership are the most deadly. The most common virus is the temptation to trim the Christian message to the world's current values. Church leaders are faced with the deconstruction of the family, preached by our intellectual elite and promoted with vigor by press, television, radio, and the Net; and they wonder how they can press the case for the Christian view of the family. It is too easy to back down in the face of what seems universal pressure. And where the church is no more than a social club, the pressure is even greater.

An able and active Christian politician told a meeting of church leaders, "Don't back down. Take your stand on traditional Christian teaching. The firmer you stand, the nearer they will have to come to your position."

However strong the arguments of the chattering classes, the majority of children still grow up in traditional families. Those who are trying to make the family work need positive support. Church leaders are pressed to be compassionate to those with different "lifestyles." Christ was compassionate to the woman "taken in adultery," but he told her, "go, and sin no more" (John 8:11, KJV).

Churches are under pressure to have good programs for their members, and wisdom has it that the churches with the best programs get the most members. But there is nothing about church programs in the parable of the sheep and the goats (Matt. 25:31-46), which tells us who will be accepted into Christ's eternal kingdom and who will not. The parable tells us,

> When the Son of Man comes in his glory and all the angels with him, he will sit on this throne in heavenly glory. All the nations will appear before him, and he will separate the people one from another as a shepherd separates the sheep from the goats (vv. 31-32).

There is little question that this parable is about the final judgment. It says nothing about good programs or even about church membership. It is all about deeds. To those he welcomes, Jesus says,

> I was hungry and you gave me something to eat, I was thirsty and you gave me something to drink, I was a stranger and you invited me in, I needed clothes and you clothed me, I was sick

and you looked after me, I was in prison and you came to visit me (vv. 35-36).

They protest that they have done nothing like this for Christ, and he says,

whatever you did for one of the least of these brothers of mine, you did for me.

To the others, he says,

whatever you did not do for one of the least of these, you did not do for me.

And he condemns them in words seldom uttered in polite churches today. A true leader has to make sure that all that Christ said—especially those things that people do not want to hear—is given equal treatment. Otherwise we are creating a god in our own image. And a good leader has to see that those in need take their place in the church programs.

It is that love for their neighbors that melted the opposition of the Roman Empire and, when the Empire was destroyed, melted the hearts of the pagan tribes, including our own ancestors. It is that love that will last when the present philosophy collapses, and meanwhile we need leaders who will stand by the faith as others have done for two thousand years before them. And they need people in their congregations who will lead from the front in our troubled secular society.

GENERAL INDEX

Aaron, 186, 187; as priest of Israel, 56
abortion, 56-57, 74, 164
Abraham, 39; tithing to Melchizedek, 46
Africa, 61, 144; African bishops and the Lambeth Conference, 69; Islamic pressure on Christians in, 69
Ahab, 89, 114
Alcoa Aluminum, 116
Anglicans, 78
Anglo-Saxon economic model, 31-32, 99, 121, 135, 152; labor laws in, 42
Arthur Andersen, 108
Asian crisis of 1997, 128, 147, 148-49, 153, 154
"Asian tigers," 140
Austria, 124

Bacon, Francis, 9, 10, 23
Balkans, 64
Bangladesh, 132
Berlin Wall, 75
Bible: and America's founding fathers, 70; translation of into vernacular languages, 8, 18
Biden, Joseph, 172
Bismarck, Otto von, 64
Bismarck, Philip von, 60
BMW, 138
Bosnia, 65
Bourbon dynasty, 78-79
Bretton Woods Agreement, 153, 155
Britain, 9, 66, 84, 101, 122-23, 129, 147; abandonment of full employment policy, 34; Cambridgeshire, 87, 88; colonies of, 63-64; constitution of, 84; Derby, 86; and economic planning, 33; election expenses in, 52; and employ-

ment, 66; and the euro, 129; and the European Union, 100-101; and the gas tax strike, 166-67; House of Commons, 52; Liverpool, 86; and merchant ships, 38; and minority parties, 84-85; and monetarism, 41; and Parliament, 78; prevention of Nazi invasion, 68; and the property boom of the 1970s, 121-22; and the scientific method, 23; and trade deficits, 11, 39, 40, 42, 122-23, 135; union membership in, 191
British Aluminum Company, 116-17
Bush, George H. W., 40-41
Bush, George W., 53
business: and competition, 14, 93-97; and cooperation, 97-99; and government/industry relations, 99-102; and litigation, 109; need for moral moorings, 14, 119-22; and regulation, 67. *See also* trust
Butterfield, Herbert, 23

Calvin, John, 8, 19; Bible commentaries of, 8
Calvinists, 22, 78
Cambridge University, 87; and the electronic economy, 160
Canada, 124
capitalism: global, 128; and religion, 38-42
Catherwood, Fred, 13; accountant training of, 182; and Cambridge rowing discipline, 30; CEO experience, 43, 99, 115-17; as chair of the British Overseas Trade Board, 103, 150; as chair of a lumber company, 119; and church

Scripture Index